# Go with me on this...

Thirty-two short articles by an old bloke having a bit of a rant.

By
Jonathan Posner

Published by Winter & Drew Publishing Ltd



ISBN: 9781739184933

# JONATHAN POSNER

Jonathan is a full-time author living in the South West UK, writing action adventure stories set in Tudor England.

As an old bloke, he finds himself increasingly baffled by the modern world.

So in April 2022 he took to the Substack blogging platform to write a weekly article expressing his bewilderment.

The blog is called **5 Minute Break**, with short weekly articles intended to challenge and amuse.

Subjects range from an inability to comprehend the weird new norms in society, to Jonathan's incredulity at the increasingly bizarre stories in the news. He also returns frequently to the topic that confuses him the most – why it is that in the 21st century, people still cling to bronze-age religions?

This book brings together thirty-two of his articles. They are perfect if you have five minutes to spare, and just want to be challenged or, hopefully, amused. Especially if you agree with Jonathan that it's all so confusing…

For more information, visit Jonathan's author website at
https://jonathanposnerauthor.com

WINTER & DREW PUBLISHING

www.winteranddrew.com

# CONTENTS

# Go with me on this...

**Articles first published on Substack on the blog:**

5minute break

Life, the universe and other quick reads from author Jonathan Posner

**WARNING:**
This book contains strong personal opinions, strident atheism, and some profanities. If you find these offensive, please put the book down, step back and walk away.

# Introduction

Back in April 2022, I decided to start a blog channel on Substack.

**5 Minute Break** came out of one simple aim – to allow me, as an old British codger, to sound off about all the crappy things that were bothering me about the state of modern society. A largely futile exercise in 'fings-ain't-wot-they-used-to-be-ism'. An excuse to roll out a few 'WTF?' cliches.

And in all of these, my tongue was very firmly in my cheek – just a bit of a chuckle on a Monday morning for those with a similar outlook.

But eventually I started to run low on my 'and another thing' rant topics. So more and more I kept coming back to one particular subject; one that seems to be an evergreen source of endless incredulity – religion.

As someone who sees no need for any form of religion in order to behave with empathy and morality towards others, I have been constantly amazed at how faith continues to exert such a hold over people. That is particularly because we now live in an age of science and reason; one that clearly refutes any factual basis to support the major religions.

And before you say, 'yeah, right, whatever,' and wander off to do something more interesting, I would only ask that you see if perhaps we're on the same page, and

go with me on this?

# Part 1

# Go with me on modern life...

# One – The Zombie invasion

April 28th 2022

It was ever thus – the older generation complaining about the behaviour of the young.

Certainly my parents did so as I was growing up in the 1970s and 80s, and I now find myself doing exactly the same.

(I do accept that with the dreadful things going on in the world right now, my complaint does rather pale into insignificance. But anyway, here goes…)

What is it, I want to know, that is so overwhelmingly, so all-consumingly, so mind-blowingly important that people think it is perfectly OK to walk along the street not looking where they are going, but instead staring down at their phone with total absorption?

I believe they are called ‘Phone Zombies’ and I reckon in my daily walks through my home city centre I encounter at least ten or twelve of them; people (usually under 30 but sometimes older), walking confidently along the pavement through heavy foot traffic, their noses buried deep in their screens, completely, totally and utterly oblivious to those around them.

Is it an indication of the self-centric nature of our society, that as they are not looking where they are going, so it is the oncoming pedestrian’s responsibility to get out of their way?

I certainly have to dodge a fair few of these zombies every day, and each one adds another brick to the growing wall of frustration and annoyance that I have built up on this topic (does it show…?).

Perhaps I can put in a brief point of smug self-justification here… If I think of something I need to check on my phone while I am out walking, or it pings with a message, then do you know what I do? I pull over to the side of the pavement and I stop. Then, when I have finished looking at my phone, I put it away and resume my walk. I realise I am out of step with modern society, where the latest Instagram post or WhatsApp text is clearly more important than consideration for other pavement users, but hey, just call me old-fashioned…

However, back to these ‘Phone Zombies’. As each one goes past, I turn my head and give them what I believe Paddington Bear called a ‘hard stare’. This is of course, completely wasted and they continue to make their way along the street, scattering responsible citizens like an ice-breaker ploughing through an Antarctic sea. The only benefit is that it makes me feel as if I have responded in some way.

Another factor is that I am a very fast walker, and I find slow movers who hold me up highly frustrating. So anyone ambling in front of me with their attention firmly fixed on their phone is going to feel the full force of my passive-aggression as I stride past, glancing angrily at their screen to see just what could possibly be so vital that it is worth making me 'step on the brakes' and 'shift down a gear or two' as I walk.

If I approach from the front I watch to see if they do that little 'eye flick' upwards, which I assume would enable them to see where they are going. But mostly they seem to be navigating by what I can only assume is a superpower-level of peripheral vision. Unless, of course, there's an app I haven't yet come across, which makes use of a special camera built into the top of the latest phones that points forward at an angle Maybe the camera sends a little 'picture in picture' to the screen, showing the pavement ahead. Very useful if you want to keep up with important texts about tonight's pub crawl, without needing to break your stride (*at time of writing, my phone was a seven year-old model, so didn't qualify. But then again, my new one doesn't have this feature either*).

The Government has understandably taken a very dim view of people looking at their phones when driving, as the consequences of a moment's inattention can be catastrophic for both the individual driver and for other road users. While I accept that distracted walking is clearly a lesser risk, my concern is that it will only take one zombie to step out into the path of an oncoming car, or one to collide with a pedestrian with a weak heart, to make 'walking without due care and attention' into something that should be actively policed.

Meanwhile, I continue to stride and dodge and stare ineffectively as I go about my daily walks through the crowded city centre pavements, hoping that maybe one day I will get to see a Phone Zombie bounce off a lamp-post, or do a comedy pratfall over a street bench, thus validating my view that society is falling apart and things ain't what they used to be….

# Two - Crossing America on 9/11

April 28th 2022

Those of us of a certain age will tell you exactly where we were and what we were doing when the World Trade Center was attacked in September 2001. Many people in the UK will talk of being called to the office or home TV to watch the dreadful scenes unfolding in New York.

I, on the other hand, was sitting in an aeroplane in Cleveland, Ohio that sunny morning, waiting to take off and fly to Kansas City on a 4-day business trip.

We had been delayed boarding for around 45 minutes due to a technicality, otherwise we would already have been in the air when the hijacked planes hit the Twin Towers, but as it was we had only just boarded. I remember clearly sitting down, securing my belt and idly flicking through the in-flight magazine when the captain came on the Tannoy.

"Sorry, folks, but we have just been advised that there has been an incident in New York, so unfortunately we have been grounded by the Federal Aviation Authority. I have to ask you all to disembark and return to the terminal."

Coming on top of the earlier delay, this announcement was greeted with a certain amount of annoyance. Initially nobody moved – as if by staging a sit-in protest, we could force the captain to reconsider. "Aw shucks, folks," he might say, "if you really want me to, maybe I could stick two fingers up at the FAA, and sneak over to Kansas City under the radar… Whaddya reckon?"

But no, after a few seconds there was a collective resigned sigh, then everyone stood up and retrieved their hand luggage, before shuffling off the plane, muttering that nothing could possibly be so bad in New York that it could ground a plane in Cleveland…

Bear in mind that at that point we knew nothing of the incident – all we knew was that it had stopped us taking off. As we got back into the crowded terminal, nobody there seemed to know what was happening either. People were milling about, asking anyone who looked like they might have information, but all we found out was that it had been some sort of terrorist incident – although we now understood that it had been a major one.

My objectives at that point were: (a) retrieve my suitcase and (b), find a way to get to Kansas City. The first of these proved a lot more difficult than expected. We were directed to Arrivals, where occasional carousels kicked into life, spat out a suitcase or two, then ground to a halt. Eventually it became clear that the worthy folk at John Hopkins Airport were unable to unload any planes at all, and that I would need to abandon my luggage.

Meanwhile, I was also pursuing my second objective; working my way round the crowds to find another passenger going to KC. I thought perhaps we could hire a car together and share the drive.

Someone said they thought 'that fellow over there' was headed that way, so I drifted across to a gingery chap with a beard, and asked him.

"Sure," he said.

"Cool," I answered, then asked, "where are you from?"

"Libya."

"Back in a moment," I said, then slid off.

Eventually I got chatting to a girl who had been on my original flight from London. Her dad was driving up from Dayton, Ohio to pick her up. Dayton was on my route, so I cadged a lift. We then found someone who lived in Cleveland and was driving off the airport, so we got a ride to the Ramada Inn just off the Interstate. It was there that we had lunch and saw the towers coming down on TV, so then we understood the full scale of the attack.

The girl's dad arrived, had a coffee and a comfort break, then we set off. On the way we discussed the day's events, with the Americans being almost unable to comprehend how they could be subjected to a terrorist outrage on this scale. Perhaps my experience of seeing IRA attacks on the TV in the 70s and 80s gave me a different perspective, and we had an interesting discussion on the three hour drive.

They dropped me at the Avis car rental in Dayton, and I climbed into the only car that was still available, which I seem to recall was a silver Pontiac Trans Am. As night fell, I pointed its nose west and drove through cities like St. Louis and Indianapolis, enjoying the deep rumble of its muscle-car engine. I had the radio on, and was amazed by the way the Americans covered the news, with such gems as interrupting an interview with Mayor Rudy Giuliani, to bring me a news item on… an interview with Rudy Giuliani. Or cutting to an ad break after a harrowing story on the casualties, with an insensitively placed ad for ‘Bob’s Auto Sale – get your 2001 Cadillac sedan with $$$s off!’

It was around 2am when I rolled into Kansas City, and around 3am when I finally found my hotel (these were the days before widespread sat navs or smart phones – and you needed a tri-band phone to work in the States, which I didn’t have).

“I’ve made it,” I said to the night receptionist.

He looked at his computer. “But sir,” he said, looking at me suspiciously. “I have you already checked in and asleep in the room.”

“I can assure you I am not,” I said, in no mood to argue. “Whoever is in my room, it certainly isn’t me. I have just driven all the way from Ohio and I am very tired.”

Eventually we cleared the confusion, and I got to my room. I rang my wife in the UK, where it was after 9am.

“WHERE… HAVE… YOU… BEEN?!”

I told her my story, and that without a mobile it had been impossible to call her (I had tried in the airport, at the Ramada Inn and at a gas station on the road, but not been able to connect). She had apparently been calling the CEO of my company, telling him to get me home. I understand he pointed out that (a) they didn’t know where I was, (b) they had no means of contacting me, and (c) the only way back was either by boat out of New York (not happening), or by plane (definitely not happening).

When the trip was over, my luggage and I had an emotional reunion at Kansas City Airport, before I boarded one of the first flights to leave the US on schedule. Again, we had just sat down, when the captain came on the Tannoy. “I just want to let you folks know that I have a wife and kids back home, and I have every intention of returning to them. I can assure you that I will get this plane safely to London. You have my word.”

My, how we cheered.

# Three – All I want is World Peace

So don’t try to stop me, Mr Bond

October 3rd 2022

***“Welcome to my lair, Mr Bond. I will now reveal my heinous plan to take over the world, before inexplicably leaving you alone so you can use your exploding pen to destroy both my lair and my evil plan, as well as dispose of all my boiler-suited minions while you’re at it.”***

It’s a standard trope in action stories that anyone who wants to rule the world must be irredeemably evil, and that any such plan would mean misery for all. And because they are always foiled at the last possible moment, we rarely, if ever, get to see what the outcome would be if they had actually succeeded.

But in the light of the massive own-goal by the UK Government a couple of weeks ago (*the disastrous mini budget by Liz Truss and Kwasi Kwarteng*), as well as other world events this year, I have been wondering if some form of higher authority sitting above all world governments might not actually be a good thing. Sort of Europe, the IMF (the monetary one, not the one off Mission Impossible), the International Court of Justice and the United Nations all rolled into one global body. Although unlike the United Nations, it would actually have the power to make any government that steps out of line step back in again. I'm not sure how it would be constituted, how it would be elected, and how it could be made accountable, but go with me on this. For the sake of this article, let's also give it a name. I'm proposing 'Top Dog' - for no other reason than it sounds good.

So how would Top Dog function?

Firstly, it would have ultimate authority over every government in the world. Every government. Without exception. Then it would have a set of articles that govern its own actions - a sort of 'mission and vision' if you like. These would primarily be 'world peace' and 'environmental sustainability', but I'm sure some others can be brainstormed as well.

So let's look at some examples of how it might work. Let's say a large country – I don't know, Russia perhaps – decides that a neighbouring country has no right to its own sovereignty and should come under its control. Let's call this country 'Ukraine' for the purposes of this example, although I am sure others in the region could be just as applicable.

The Russians start massing troops near the border and it soon becomes clear that they are planning to invade. The worthy folk at Top Dog do some projections of possible outcomes. They decide that the impact on food supplies and energy prices will be catastrophic for much of the global population, not to mention the environment. They also factor in the impact on innocent Ukrainians, with death, destruction and mass refugee migration being the likely outcome.

"We can't have this sort of thing," they say. "We can't have global instability caused by the hubris of one man and his cheerleaders in the Kremlin." So they issue an edict that it will not go ahead, and they declare the regime in Russia to be acting beyond its remit. On this basis they then order a change of regime, requiring one that is prepared to comply with the Top Dog 'world peace' mission and vision.

Or another example. A small country, but one with an influential economy, decides to implement a policy that is so clearly bonkers, so obviously self-destructive, that it threatens to undermine the whole market economy of that country, and therefore have a domino effect across other global economies (and if you think it would not have, remember how the US sub-prime lending policy sparked the 2008 global recession). The Top Dog people get together and agree that this is not just bonkers, but it's irresponsible too. An order goes out to the relevant government that they either need to reverse the policy or step aside in favour of people who will reverse it. Crisis averted and normal service resumed (*which is, of course, pretty much what did happen*).

One final example; a regime that is so driven by religious dogma that they literally kill women for putting their clothes on 'wrong'. I think we would all agree that Top Dog should flex its muscles on this one, and substitute such religious nut-jobs with a government fit for the 21st century, before more people get hurt, or worse.

So, could Top Dog work?

We're now a global community, with everyone instantly connected to everyone else. What happens in Ukraine, UK and Iran is immediately known in every other country. We're no longer a culturally diverse world, but now truly a 'global village' where people travel widely and cultures are gradually converging. Kids are growing up in a fluidly connected world, and I think it will only be a few generations before nations are seen as a historical curiosity, with people identifying themselves as global rather than local. Especially as they will need to move to geographical locations where the environment still supports life. In such a case, it makes sense for there to be a single overall authority, making decisions for the common good.

I know, I know - it's all hopelessly idealistic, impossible to implement in reality, and it's hard to see how its decisions could be enforced, but as I said, go with me on the principle of the thing. Wouldn't it be great to know that when it comes to governments, there are some responsible adults in the room, ready, willing and able to make the kids behave?

In the old days kings took their authority from God - who's 'will' was open to multiple interpretations, so this was divisive in the extreme. Replacing it with an authority that has both singularity and clarity must, by definition, be better. Not only that, but it would knock the conspiracy theorists on the head – there really would be a global elite in overall charge. The only difference is that we would know about them, and they would have some form of accountability for their actions.

***"What is that, Mr. Bond? You want to stop my plan for peaceful global domination? With your pen? I think we need to re-frame our perspective here, Mr. Bond."***

# Four - My opinion is important

If only to me.

August 29th 2022

I had an interesting dream last night, which I would like to share.

Now, I know what you're thinking – other people's dreams are usually only interesting to themselves, and the freedom from any rules or conventions makes them contextually hard to follow (…and then this green viking turned into a fish and dived into the pink sea after the swimming laptop…). I get that, but my point is that a dream can sometimes spark an idea – and this one did exactly that.

The idea for this article, naturally.

I don't usually remember my dreams for more than a few seconds after I awake (if that), but this was a particularly vivid one, and stayed with me in some detail. I suspect that I also woke up right in the middle of REM (the sleep state not the pop group), which also helps with recall. The dream itself was very simple. I was working in an office – the headquarters of some faceless multinational corporate (OK, so maybe it was closer to being a nightmare). The point is that I knew I had all the answers – the right marketing strategy, the perfect HR policies and so on, but every time I tried to explain these to my colleagues, I was shut down with a comment that such thinking was not needed right now, thank-you very much. At one point I even tried to get a colleague to one side to explain my thinking in a one-to-one, but we couldn't find a quiet space alone, until we came across the CEO's office and it was empty. I was part-way though explaining my thoughts to the colleague, when we were interrupted by the CEO, who had apparently been sitting at his desk all along. He then explained that all the ideas I was setting out were – how should he put it? '…my opinions only, and not aligned with their wider plan…'

I woke up with a burning sense of injustice and frustration. How dare my colleagues be so dismissive and condescending? How could they not value my contribution when I had all the answers? Why was I not being heard? But once I had been through the whole 'it's only a dream' thing, I got to thinking.

Maybe the message my subconscious was giving me here was how a single person's opinion can be marginal, when viewed against the wider scope of a complex problem.

It made me realise how we as a society so often filter complicated issues through the simplistic viewpoint of a single person's experience. In essence, how we try and use 'human interest' stories to illustrate issues that deserve a much more in-depth and nuanced approach.

Take for example, the current appalling increase in the cost of living – and the cost of energy in particular. Everyone is suffering, and as the prices go up, it is only going to get much, much worse. As I flick through the news channels, I find they are all using ‘human interest’ stories to illustrate the issue. But I think that’s missing the point. To hear from some bloke who’s been ambushed in the street by a TV crew that he’s unable to pay his gas bill does not, in my opinion, advance our overall understanding of the situation. Such views might be of interest to the bloke himself and possibly to his mates down the pub, but they are way too simplistic and personal to advance the national understanding of highly complex issues.

Instead I think we should be looking at the root causes of the inflation – including causes such as:

- The end of the pandemic
- Putin’s wholly unsupportable war in Ukraine
- The world’s reliance on dwindling fossil fuels
- Brexit

And we should be considering how the trajectory of these issues will create change in the future – so that we can get a perspective on what the eventual outcomes will be. I’m sorry, but I don’t think hearing how Bert from Birmingham is going to manage his finances cuts it (any more than a story on how Teresa in Taunton felt isolated during the pandemic illustrated the socio-economic effects of COVID).

And while I am on the subject of the cost of living, I do take my hat off to the Labour Party, who have continually banged on about how the energy companies (and the train companies and the postal companies, for that matter) have been paying dividends to shareholders rather than passing on profits to the customers as lower prices, or to the workers as higher pay. They are re-framing the narrative so it sounds like a few fat cats are raking off the money that could benefit the many – while the truth is that a large chunk of these dividends are actually paid into peoples’ pensions and other funds that help keep the economy afloat. Not to mention that without shareholder investment (and the expectations of a return) such companies would be unable to trade – affecting both customer well-being and employee livelihoods.

So I felt my dream was worth sharing, if only to show how I came to realise that 'human interest' stories are marginal to a deeper understanding of complex issues. Sadly, I can't see how putting Bert from Birmingham or Teresa from Taunton on the spot have contributed anything of value to the solution of our modern-day problems. Of course, if we were to put Vladimir from Moscow on the spot (a war crimes court in the Hague, perhaps?) then there's one individual who's life changes could have much wider implications.

Now ***that*** would be a dream worth having.

# Five - Don't ask me

No seriously, don't ask me.

10th October 2022

**This article expands on the previous article – that of 'vox-pop' street interviews on TV news programmes.**

In my humble (and oft-repeated) opinion, TV news stories that feature street interviews represent not only the worst kind of lazy journalism, but they are almost always completely irrelevant because the interviewee has no real understanding of the issue. I say '***almost*** always' because I suppose there might be a remote statistical possibility that a journalist and a cameraman may stumble upon a member of the public who not only understands the subject in question, but is also well-informed enough to give a coherent answer. I think it is much more likely that the person being quizzed – worthy though they no doubt are – will have an opinion that's relevance is inversely proportionate to the complexity and nuance of the issue. Their personal view may be fascinating to them and to their close family, but sadly it gives little, if any, real insight to the viewer.

I thought I might use this article to illustrate my point in a bit more detail – sharing with you my own ill-informed and simplistic views on topics that I know very little about. A sort of ***can't beat 'em, join 'em*** kind of thing. So here are some of my questionable opinions on the hot topics of the day:

**Reporter** Excuse me sir. I am doing a few pieces for the evening news. I'd like to start with the Ukraine war. I wonder if I can ask how you think this could be brought to an end?

**Me** Oh yes, that's simple. Putin can't be seen to lose face, so however badly the war goes, and however much he wants a way out, he won't end the conflict himself. He will let it rumble on, continuing to lie to the Russian population with ever hollower victory stories, until eventually it is clear even to them that he has lost this war. Then he has two options. The first is to claim victory anyway and make a 'tactical withdrawal' – which means he will almost certainly be hounded from office and face some kind of repercussion for his actions.

**Reporter** And the second?

**Me** He nukes Kyiv and we're all fucked.

**Reporter** That's bleak. Any other options?

**Me** I am glad you asked that. Yes, there is one clear way out of this, and it relies on Kremlin insiders realising that the world sees this as Putin's war. So if they stage a coup and throw Putin in jail, they can then withdraw from Ukraine, sue for peace and blame the whole thing on him. The Russian people can also put clear distance between themselves and the war, because it was all down to one man, and now he's gone. The new regime can restore relations with the West, and the world can breathe a little easier.

**Reporter** Thank you. You seem well informed on this.

**Me** Yeah, sorry about that.

**Reporter** OK, let's move on to the USA. Do you think the Republicans will make gains in the mid-term elections?

**Me** Wow – that's a good one. I hope not, because the Republican party appears to be a bunch of christo-fascist weirdos intent on dragging America back to the bronze-age. I mean, anyone who believes that life should be lived according to a book that promotes such immoral acts as incest, genocide, rape, slavery, child sacrifice and misogyny is not someone who should be in charge of anything. These people glorify ignorance as much as they glorify guns, and actively teach against scientific learning. If the Americans give them any more slack than they already have, who knows where it may end? At least their spiritual leader, who some might call an orange-faced man-baby, seems to be losing influence. I suppose that's something.

**Reporter** Er, right… Iran?

**Me** Another very good example of why medieval theists should kept out of government.

**Reporter** OK. The cost-of-living crisis?

**Me** Let's be clear – this is a world issue, not limited to the UK Government alone. The fact that the UK Government has responded to it by appearing to make it worse, proves that policy should be driven by common-sense pragmatism rather than ideology.

**Reporter** Thank you for your opinions. I'm not sure that they add any real insight, but interesting, nonetheless.

**Me** Well, there you go. I'm just some bloke you stopped in the street. What did you expect?

# Six - Don't look that way

It's not natural.

5th September 2022

Those who know me well will confirm that I am not a fan of so called 'reality' TV. I genuinely don't give a flying fuck what happens on Love Island, or which faded 'celeb' wants someone to get them out of there. I have belly-button fluff that means more to me than all the Kardashians put together, and I neither know nor care who is singing or dancing from under a mask. Whatever goes on in Chelsea leaves me cold, and the only way in Essex is out onto the east coast, to the glorious open marshlands and river where I grew up. And as for Big Brother and Married at First Sight – if I wanted to see plastic people pulling on each other's strings, then believe me, I would find an episode of Thunderbirds. At least the cast look more realistic.

In the office where I used to work before I became a full-time author, Love Island dominated the conversation when it was on – something to do with who was seeing who, and what the other contestants thought – although I will admit I did try and tune out the chat, so I may be wrong. But it was a standing joke that as soon as this topic of conversation started, then Jonathan would roll his eyes to the ceiling and type very loudly on his keyboard as a form of diversionary tactic (although excessively loud typing is actually a core skill of mine – I even manage to get occasional blood blisters under my fingertips).

What has happened to our society, that we have become so obsessed with people who have nipped, tucked and tattooed themselves into identikit grotesques? I know it is the perennial cry of the old codger, but when did our standards of acceptable beauty change, so that women with perma-surprised eyes and lips like bathroom plungers became the norm? And when did it become *de rigeur* to get 'inked' – with anything from a small 'ankle motif', to images emerging up the neck and trying to take over the face, like some ghastly creeping triffid? I have no doubt that having at least 30% of your body covered in 'tats' is the minimum entry requirement for appearing on shows like Love Island or Married at First Sight – although as I have never seen a single second of either, that is just my guess.

And don't get me started on these shiny multi-coloured talons that seem all the rage now. Why do women think it is OK to sport the kind of nails that would make a velociraptor chitter with fear and run the other way? I mean, it's the practicalities that get me – A&E departments must be awash with people who got an itch on their nose, then had their eye out as collateral damage.

Am I the only one who still thinks that 'natural' is the ideal in human beauty, and that any attempt to change what nature has given us is inevitably going to result in less beauty rather than more? Of course, I do know that one only sees the effects of things like plastic surgery, botox and fillers when the results are painfully obvious. There are probably people out there who have paid a fortune to achieve a more subtle and 'natural' look (i.e. the 'natural' look they might have had twenty years before) – and if it has worked, then you don't spot it. It's a bit like the men who wear a toupé – when it is badly done it stands out like a fart in a lift. But if it is expertly done, then you pass the bloke in the street in happy ignorance, never actually clocking that he's sporting a syrup.

But the sad fact is that so many people have these procedures done, and in such a way that it is clearly visible – that it now seems to be the norm. So I have decided that the time has come to push back; to make a stand. It's time to stop glorifying surgery and to celebrate all that is wonderfully natural about human appearance, as well ageing gracefully.

I want us to accept with glad joyfulness when a man's hair migrates away from the top of his head and sprouts instead in great clumps out of his ears and nose (mine certainly does, and it grows back indecently fast if I try and trim it). Let's not give a single toss about having a saggy neck, baggy eyes or a jowly chin. Let us celebrate these as things of beauty, and rejoice in the fact that we are maturing nicely. After all, a fine wine improves with age – why can we not do the same?

I'm even thinking of pitching a reality show to the networks. It's going to be called Love Creaks, and feature a bunch of older folk marooned on an island together. They have to decide who makes the best bridge partner, or maybe the ideal tea-brewer, then cosy up for warm evenings in front of the Antiques Roadshow. Naturally anyone with a tattoo or who has 'had some work done' would not be eligible, and anyone left standing at the end would be declared the winner. I think it has the older demographic written all over it, and I for one, would discuss the finer points with colleagues after each episode.

Naturally.

# Seven - You have to respect my rights

Because I'm worth it.

1st August 2022

In the first article in this book I broached the subject of phone zombies – those people who insist on walking along crowded streets with their noses so deeply buried in their phones that they are apparently oblivious to where they are going. My point was that as they are not looking, then it becomes necessary for the more responsible citizens who are walking towards them to get out of their way, or shout to alert them.

I would now like to expand on this, and use these Phone Zombies to illustrate a wider point – that as a society, I believe we are becoming increasingly self-centred. Indeed, it seems to me that we're going well beyond mere self-centredness and have arrived at an altogether more insidious place. A place called 'self-entitlement.' A place where anyone who wants to act in a selfish way can do so, despite the negative impact their behaviour might have on others. Indeed, any resulting unpleasantness is the other person's fault for trying to thwart their self-expression.

Take these phone zombies as an example. When I challenged one after I had had to step out into the road to avoid his meanderings, I got a mouthful of abuse. 'How dare I,' he seemed to be saying (I didn't hang around to catch the exact words, so I am speculating a bit here), 'how dare I tell him to watch where he was going? I was abusing his right to look at his phone while he was walking, and the mere fact that I had to step into the road was my effing fault, not his.'

Perhaps this same chap was in an Audi A3 that tried to pull into my lane on the M5 recently, causing me to have to brake hard and hit the horn. If I interpret the single finger sign he gave me out of the window correctly, before he sped off at well over 70mph, then it was my fault for being in his way, rather than his for not looking as he pulled out.

A couple of further examples, neither of which need much elaboration: people who don't pick up their dog's mess (or hang a bag of the foul stuff on a tree – what's that all about?), people who eat noisily, and those who talk or look at their phones in the theatre.

How have we got to this place? As a writer of Tudor-era historical fiction, it is tempting to say that it is merely a continuation of the entitlement previously felt only by the nobility and landed classes – but now democratised to all members of society. And I am sure there's an element of truth in that – but I think it goes further. Maybe it's the weakening of the influence of the church on society. But if you look at the church's use of entitlement to protect its own position – from the Inquisition all the way to today's US Christian fundamentalism

– then that argument doesn't hold. Indeed, the church's persecution complex when challenged on its dogmatic insistence that everyone has to live by its moral code, seems to me to be the very definition of self-entitlement.

No, I think the blame lies with *consumerism* in general, and *marketing* in particular.

"Whoa there, Jonathan!" you might interject here, "are you lurching to the left? Are you becoming a bit of a socialist in your old age?"

"Well, no," I would reply, "I still think that the overall freedoms of a capitalist society far outweigh the necessary restrictions of socialism, but hear me out on this."

Consumerism means offering in essence what the buyer wants (or in the case of Apple, what the buyer didn't actually know they wanted, but do now). So companies are only successful if they meet the desires of the consumer. And as the existence of a thriving market research industry demonstrates, companies will spend vast sums of money finding out exactly what those desires are. So we're a society where the needs of the individual are not only respected, but they are also actually *worshiped* – at the altar of consumerism.

Which is where marketing comes in. In the old days, this was conducted on a one-to-many model – where a single producer of goods or services shouted their wares by advertising to anyone who would listen (usually a large – and therefore diverse – segment of consumers). As receivers of this advertising, we recognised that we were not seen as individuals – so we were less likely to feel any sense of self-entitlement as a result.

But now marketing has recognised that we really are a much more diverse bunch, and each of us is in a mini-segment of one. So even though mass-targeted advertising does still happen, the internet has enabled a new 'sharp-end' of modern marketing that works on a one-to-one model – with each of us being served marketing content over the internet based on our individual buying and viewing habits. OK, it can sometimes get it spectacularly wrong – such as the recent spate of ads I have been getting on Instagram for private jet hire – but in essence we are now having our very own individual needs and desires heard by companies, all falling over themselves to offer us the mix of products and services that is wholly unique to us as individuals.

And if that does not make us feel self-entitled, I don't know what does.

# Eight - Future classics?

Passing on the baton of Rock.

July 11th 2022

As a Tudor history buff, I do like to get out and experience the Tudor world. So I was pleased to be able to attend a very entertaining classical music concert a few weeks ago, featuring a counter-tenor singing 16th and 17th century songs in a Tudor-era priory. Then last week I had the opportunity to see a very talented international harpist playing music from the 16th through 19th centuries in beautiful old village church.

Both performers gave illuminating short talks between each piece, covering the historical background, a bit about the composers, and telling us how the songs came to be written. The counter-tenor introduced several of his songs by telling us that although these were the popular pieces of the day, the establishment of the time may have thought them a little risqué. He also pointed out that as we were in a 16th century hall (preserved in all its Tudor glory), there was every chance that the songs we were hearing could actually have been performed in this very place over 400 years ago. It sent a shiver down my spine to think that I was being treated to a very similar experience to the one our Tudor ancestors would have enjoyed – hearing the same music in pretty much the same environment. OK, maybe not my ancestors, as they would have been too busy ploughing fields in Poland at the time – but you get the point.

This then got me thinking.

Surely, if the logic is followed, then the music played today will be the 'historical classics' of the future? After all, I remember a DJ joking in the late 1970s when punk was on the rise (and being censured for explicit lyrics), that as Radio 2 was mainly playing the hits of 20 years earlier, then in 20 years' time they would be playing 'classic' punk as 'nostalgia'. But sure enough, I do seem to recall Radio 2 giving us the soothing tones of 'God Save the Queen' by the Sex Pistols sometime in the Noughties. And given that as I write, Kate Bush is once again running up the hill to the top of the charts, then it does seem to me that what goes round comes round.

But will such music still be played 400 years from now? And if it is, who knows which works will have stood the test of time and how it will be received. After all, if what may have been a bit risqué in the 1580s is now seen as totally establishment, what's to say the same might not happen in the next 400 years?

Picture if you will, an audience settling back at a classical concert in the year 2422. The guitars tune up; the drummer gives a few trial beats, then the conductor taps his baton on the music stand and turns to the audience.

"Now this next number was popular in the urban environment of London in the early part of the 21st century," he'll say, "and it's a piece of classic grime. Grime emerged originally as a development of UK Garage, Jungle and Hip-Hop. This song is by one of the leading proponents of the genre, Lethal Bizzle, who was noted mainly as the MC of the More Fire Crew. I invite you now to sit back, relax, and enjoy his outstanding piece, 'Oi!'

Or maybe it will be other examples of our current musical works that endure? "And now," our future conductor might say once the Lethal Bizzle song is over and the polite applause has faded away, "our next piece comes from a leading ensemble of the late 20th and early 21st century called ABBA. Of course, much of their work may already be familiar to you, as I believe the ABBA Voyage virtual concert is now booking until 2472, but here is a rarely-heard work from the 1976 album 'Arrival', called 'Dum Dum Diddle'. Listen for the seminal chorus line 'Dum Dum Diddle, To Be Your Fiddle' and consider how this has influenced so much of the classical music that subsequently emerged over the next two hundred years. Songs such as 'De Do Do Do De Da Da Da,' and of course, 'Radio Gaga' are fine early examples of this lyrical genre."

Or maybe it will be other works that survive – who knows? But if any do, then I hope my distant descendants and classical music buffs appreciate the musical heritage we are handing down.

Lennon and McCartney, anyone?

# Nine - Now where was I?

28th April 2022

I will come clean and admit it - I have a very poor short term memory.

We're talking at the level of an absent-minded goldfish here.

But in the age of Google and smartphones, where the function of memory has been delegated to 1s and 0s on a silicon chip, is that really such a bad thing?

Back in the 1980s I was a salesman for an exhibition stand company. I had on my desk a Rolodex (you might want to google that, kids), with the phone numbers of all my prospects and customers. If you threw any one of around 15 or 20 customer names at me, I could rattle off their phone number no problem. I phoned them regularly and their numbers became burned into my short term memory. If I was not next to my Rolodex – maybe in a phone box (remember those?), then such wide recall was not only invaluable, it was necessary. I didn't want to carry my

Rolodex around, or transcribe the numbers into a phone book, either. So I relied on my prodigious memory.

Or if I drove anywhere once, and knew I would need to find my way there again, then I would easily memorise it, turn by turn, street name by street name, so I could navigate the next time without any mistakes.

And as a salesman, I knew how important it was to listen actively and remember names, so I could build relationships and sales.

Fast forward to the present day, and it's a whole different story. Now I struggle to remember where I put my keys, let alone memorise a phone number (beyond my own mobile), and if I need to drive somewhere, I use the sat nav every time – meaning I couldn't tell you the route I'd taken even if I had just arrived. And that's not counting the number of mistakes I'd have made en-route, where one turning on the screen looks much like another.

And although I still try and listen actively and remember names, I do find it a real struggle, unless the person has a physical characteristic that reminds me of someone I know well.

Is it an age thing? I know memory gets poorer as we get older, but maybe it's a double whammy – a combination of increasing years and less and less use of memory in everyday situations? Maybe memory is like a muscle – if you don't use it, you lose it. And as we don't need to use it anywhere near as much as we used to, we're losing it. I mean, if you want to remember something these days, it's a case of needing only to remember one thing - where to find the information. Is it on Facebook or WhatsApp? Was it in a post on LinkedIn? Or is it something you can quickly google? Although to be fair, I can become a tad bewildered if I can't remember which platform a message came in on, especially if it's on my phone.

I often find myself waking up in the middle of the night, struggling to remember some inconsequential bit of trivia. All six characters in *Friends*? The original seven Mercury astronauts? The names and nicknames of each Spice Girl? No problem, just reach for the phone and google it. Although strangely enough I can tell you without resorting to my phone that Jim Jacobs and Warren Casey wrote *Grease*, and Jerry Bock, Sheldon Harnick and Joseph Stein wrote *Fiddler on the Roof* (feel free to google that one as well, kids). At least there's some trivia I can recall – although that pales into insignificance, compared to what I used to be able to remember. Indeed, there was once a time where no-one in my family would play Trivial Pursuit with me, as I could bring out some random fact from the back of my head, and astound them with my ability to answer the most obscure question. My then wife was truly gobsmacked when I correctly answered a question with the answer '*The Rubaiyat of Omar Khayyam*' – not only had she never heard of it, but she could not believe that I had either, or even knew what it was. To this day she still thinks I cheated (I didn't - I just darned well remembered it).

I suppose ultimately we will end up with some chip implant taking over the function of memory completely. We will then be able to google the answer to any obscure question without picking up our phone or even twiddling our thumbs on a screen. Our biological memory will then dwindle to nothing, but wow - our bionic memory will be phenomenal! Of course, it will probably mean the end of the pub quiz and TV game shows, as everyone will be able to operate at the level of a *Mastermind* champion, but maybe that will be a small price to pay for going back to having a good memory – and indeed even a better memory than when I could rattle off the phone numbers of 15 or 20 long forgotten 80s companies.

Now, what was it I was about to do?

# Ten - Help! I'm being ambushed by ads

20th June 2022

I want to set you a challenge.

It's fairly trivial – nothing world-changing here. I just want to see if this is an actual thing, or if it's just me. And I am perfectly prepared to accept it is just me, or even that it is purely coincidental. Go with me on this.

The thing I want to test is: how come, pretty much every time I channel-surf the commercial TV channels, I seem to land not the programme, but on the ads?

Picture the scene. I've switched on the TV, and say I have come in on BBC1. So far, so good. But say there's something showing on the Beeb that I am not interested in, like EastEnders or football. So I will idly flick over to BBC2…

Gardening.

So on to ITV. It's on the ads.

How about Channel 4? Also on the ads.

Or maybe Channel 5? Ads again.

And so on. You get the idea.

And it always seems to be that I land at the beginning of a very long ad break – so long in fact, that I have completely forgotten which programme I was expecting to see (although please see the previous article on my poor short-term memory).

When I first became sensitised to this phenomenon, I was merely amused in a wry sort of way. But over time I am beginning to wonder if it really is a thing. A statistical anomaly. An obsession, even…

Am I overthinking this? (don't answer…). Or is it just because I am truly sensitised to it? That when I land on the ads, it reinforces my perception that they follow me around the channels, like some malevolent little personal rain cloud? Which means that when I actually do land on a programme, it doesn't support my hypothesis, so it doesn't register? Or maybe it's like Schrodinger's Cat – just before I arrive, the commercial channel is happily showing their programme, but the millisecond I switch onto it, the ads come on?

Or then again, perhaps it is something to do with statistics – that a certain percentage of hourly airtime is ads, so my probability of switching over at ad-time is statistically high enough to ensure it happens very often? And there's another possibility – to do with the timing of my channel-surfing. Maybe when I swap channels after a programme is finished, I am increasing my odds of hitting the ads? That's because all the commercial channels are also between programmes.

Not that I have anything against ads, mind you. I had a long and worthwhile career in marketing before establishing myself as a full-time publisher and author, and was involved in the creation of a fair few ads myself. It's just that I want to watch the programme, not be enticed for the umpteenth time to book a family holiday (I'm single), or try a breathable memory foam mattress topper for 60 days, whether or not it has a full money-back guarantee. Incidentally, if you ever watch *Wheeler Dealers* – my Saturday morning guilty pleasure – you'll know that a mattress topper ad can somehow be spun out for the full duration of a break, which is a very long time indeed. And while I am on the subject, there's a woman who does the all-too frequent ads for a prize draw to win a £million house, who has the most condescending and annoying voice I have ever, ever heard. I am sure she's a lovely person and all that, but her voice sets my teeth on edge. Sorry, but there it is.

So here's my challenge. See if you also seem to hit the ads more often than you would statistically expect, when you surf onto a commercial TV channel. Don't keep a score, or jot it down in a notebook or anything like that, which, let's face it, would be a bit weird. No, just build an impression of whether or not the sod's law of ad breaks applies to you as much as I think it does to me. See how often you say, 'Oh no, not the ads again…' before pressing the 'channel up' button and moving from, say, a 'cinema verité' ad for home intruder alarms, to perhaps a 'slice of life' one for a bank.

And if it does now become a 'thing' for you, that takes you beyond 'wry amusement' into the realm of 'this is an obsession', then I am truly, truly sorry. Maybe it will all seem better after a good night's sleep.

In which case, how about trying a new mattress topper?

# Eleven - The true meaning of Christmas

A pagan winter celebration?

21st November 2022

Ahhh, Christmas is coming! Bringing with it cheesy ads on TV, George Michael on the radio and fake snow in shop windows.

And, of course, the sound of worthy Christians trying to hold back the fast-flowing tide of commercialism – with about as much success as King Canute on the beach.

One can only admire their dogged determination as they exhort the rest of the population to 'remember the true meaning of Christmas' – their plaintive cries almost completely drowned out by the beep of contactless payments, the doorbell rings of Amazon deliveries and the raucous noise of drunken office parties. Yet they plough bravely on, using keywords like 'nativity', 'baby Jesus' and 'church' as they try to reset the national consciousness back to some mythical golden age; one when Christmas was a purely religious festival celebrating nothing more than the birth of their saviour.

Only it is hard to pinpoint exactly when this was – if ever.

Let's start with the origins of the December 25th celebration. As I understand it, this festival started life not to commemorate the birth of the historical Jesus (if such a man ever existed – I remain to be convinced), but as a take-over of the earlier Pagan / Roman festival of Saturnalia. This itself was a celebration of the winter solstice – when the days started getting longer and the coming of spring could be anticipated. It was also the time when alcohol that had been brewed earlier in the year was now ready to drink.

Why the specific date of December 25th? There is no evidence in the gospels that this was the date of Jesus's birth – and apparently no biblical indication that such an event should even be celebrated. No, it seems that the basis for choosing it was that it was originally the end of Saturnalia (allowing for subsequent calendar adjustments). It was also the date of 'birth' of a Persian sun god called Mithras that some Romans followed, who 'emerged' at the solstice as if a child from the 'womb' of a virgin goddess called Astarte. Perhaps the early Christians absorbed these myths and festivals, transferring them to their new god, Jesus, and calling it the Feast of the Nativity? It took a few hundred years, but by the end of the sixth century the Christian festival had become firmly established, and had even reached England.

So if we fast-forward a thousand years to the deeply religious Tudor era, is this when we find a Christmas that is the unadulterated celebration of nothing more than the birthday of Jesus? Not exactly. This largely agrarian society saw Christmas not only as a religious festival, but also treated it as a break from farming in the depths of winter, and like the Saturnalians, a chance to celebrate the coming of spring. After fasting through advent, there were twelve days of feasting, drinking, gambling, play-acting, kissing under mistletoe (another pagan throwback) and the burning of a yule log (a tradition from Norse mythology). So yes, Christmas might have had the nativity at its heart, but the population could not let go of the pagan roots of the festival, nor the opportunity to have a lot of fun. It's not hard to imagine Tudor religious leaders folding their arms, tutting loudly, and observing that people really needed to 'remember the true meaning of Christmas'.

Which is sort-of what the Puritans did in the following century, by deciding that if society couldn't celebrate Christmas in a sensible and sober fashion, then they couldn't celebrate it at all. In the true spirit of ultra-religious killjoys since time immemorial, they banned it completely. Not only did this mean that Christmas was officially off the agenda until the Restoration of Charles II in 1660, but the anti-Christmas ethos also crossed the Atlantic with the puritan Pilgrim Fathers. And although other immigrants to America did observe the festival, it seems that this puritan ethic largely survived for a couple of hundred years – such that Christmas was not formally recognised as a federal holiday in the USA until 1870.

However, it was in the early 19th century that the principles of family reconciliation, gift-giving, plus trees and carols, started to gain traction – with Charles Dickens's influential *A Christmas Carol* in 1843. In America, Washington Irving's short stories of the 1820s, which were based on his experience of Christmas celebrations in England, had a similar effect. And in 1822, Clement Clarke Moore's poem *A Visit From St. Nicholas* (beginning with the line: *'Twas the Night Before Christmas'*) helped start the tradition of the giving and receiving of gifts, as it referenced a 3rd/4th century bishop in Turkey who was a secret gift-giver – known as *Sinterklaas* by the Dutch. This added another layer of myth to the whole festival, in the form of the Santa Claus / Father Christmas character. And, of course, it created the tradition of admitting to kids that Santa isn't real, while forcefully telling them that Jesus actually is.

Gift-giving created further distance from the 'baby Jesus' story by introducing seasonal Christmas shopping. This has become so integral to today's celebrations that it is surely the main reason why the current god-squaders get so worked up. As western society has become more and more driven by commercialism, this period of frenetic buying in the months (yes, *months*) up to December 25th, has become such an integral and structural element of the economy that many companies rely on it for survival.

So, do today's worthy Christians have a point when they try to get us to 'remember the true meaning of Christmas'? I don't believe so, given that when you strip away layer after layer of myth, you end up with a pagan festival of feasting and drinking; one that celebrated the turn of winter and the coming of spring. Do they mean we should celebrate Saturnalia? Worship Mithras? Find a more appropriate date for the birth of Jesus? (Think about it – do shepherds really watch their sheep in the deep midwinter?) I think not.

No, I would suggest these worthy followers of Christ go their churches and celebrate however they want, and leave the rest of us to enjoy Christmas for what it is – the latest incarnation of an ancient pagan festival, re-invented for today's commercial consumer economy.

Merry Christmas, everyone!

# Twelve - Is cash king or does it ping?

Or can it help you spend less this Christmas?

5th December 2022

I happened to walk past a Christmas market kiosk the other day, and was totally amazed by what I saw.

I don't particularly recall what it was selling – no doubt some suitably seasonal gifty stuff – but I don't remember because my eye was drawn instead to a sign that was prominently displayed.

It read 'Cash Sales Only'.

Now, I know there are always reasons for things, and no doubt the stall-holder had a particularly good one – like maybe their phone was out of signal, or the battery on their card reader was dead – but surely this must have put a serious limit on their sales?

I mean, who in their right mind would otherwise willingly restrict their market to just those who carry cash? Especially when it costs virtually nothing to set up an account with one of those online card merchants and get a card reader that takes contactless payments in the real world.

In fact, I am going to go out on a limb here, and say that it simply is not necessary to carry cash in today's contactless society. I can count on the fingers of one hand the number of times I have got the stuff out of a machine this year. (I am, of course speaking metaphorically. I am not some saddo who keeps a record of every time they take out cash. At least, not any more).

Now I know what you're going to say to this. "Jonathan, you arrogant little tit," you say, wagging your finger at me in a disapproving fashion, "not everyone is as fortunate as you to have a credit or debit card." And you would be right, of course (about the credit/debit card part, not the arrogant tit thing). But here's my point. Since Covid, we have become a contactless micro-payment society. Remember pre-pandemic, when retailers had a £5 or £10 minimum spend limit on card transactions? Well, those days are long gone, blown away by the collective social sneeze called Covid. Now we just have to wave our piece of plastic (or in my case, my phone) at the little contactless symbol, and 'ping', we've paid. Surely, therefore, cash is the exception rather than the rule? An 'outlier', as the statisticians like to say. So limiting your potential market to just these people is somewhat puzzling.

Which brings me to the main point of this article. As you start the new week, with the Christmas holiday coming up fast on the horizon, there's going to be an awful lot of 'pings' happening. Christmas food and drink? Ping. Tree and decorations? Ping ping. Gifts for everyone? Ping ping ping. A German sausage plus onions from the Christmas Market? PING! (OK that might just be me). But it's going to get expensive – and that's before you count the cost of keeping warm at home or putting fuel in your car. I know I am not saying anything new here, (as if I ever do), and we're all facing the awfulness of the cost-of-living crisis, but it's just too easy to wave your credit card at the ping-thing and suddenly find you're spending way too much.

Call me an old cynic, but it seems to me that by making contactless payments so easy, it's a licence to print money for the banks (if that's not a contradiction in terms). I read somewhere – or possibly saw it on TikTok – that lending by the banks creates money out of thin air. So the more we 'ping' our cards, the more they lend, so the more money is created. Which is not only inflationary, but also means that we, the public, end up spending money we don't have buying things we don't need, in order to keep the wheels of capitalism turning.

Now, I am no economist, so everything I said in the paragraph above may be wrong, but it sort-of hangs together. I'm going to stand by it (unless someone can show me how I am wrong – in which case I will be happy to change my view).

But in the meantime, I am coming to the conclusion that maybe cash is not such a bad idea after all. Maybe it's actually a good thing to get a certain amount out of the machine for say, one month or one week, then spend that and no more? Use it as a basic, but effective form of budget management?

In which case, no doubt, every place I go will have a sign up saying 'Card Sales Only'.

# Thirteen - Don't do that - it's bad luck!

And just how, exactly, does that work?

9th January 2023

I am writing this on 6th January, having just taken down my Christmas decorations. It didn't take me long; there was only a string of coloured lights and a few Christmas cards.

OK, just call me the Grinch. Or Scrooge. Bah, humbug, etc.

I chose today to take them down, not because it is the traditional date, or there's any religious significance for me, but because I happened to be sitting on my sofa gazing absent-mindedly at them, when I suddenly decided their time had come. Hasta la vista, decs.

As I say, there was no particular reason based on religion or tradition. It is purely coincidental that the impulse came on Jan

6th – which is, according to some, Twelfth Night, and therefore the traditional religious time to take them down (see: Church of England). Although it might not have been quite such serendipity, as there are others who say Twelfth Night is actually the 5th January, so I missed it by a day. Apparently it's all down to whether you count Christmas Day as the First Night, or start counting from the day after. Or whatever.

But the point here is that religious tradition says it is 'bad luck' to take them down after Twelfth Night.

This got me thinking. Why do we talk of 'bad luck' when you do something contrary to some superstition or tradition? Walking under ladders, new shoes on the table, broken mirrors, a single magpie – there are plenty of examples. And there are many people who will say, with a totally straight face, 'don't do [that thing], it will bring you bad luck.'

What? I mean, what? How is that supposed to work, exactly?

It has to work somehow – it can't just happen spontaneously. If you do something that everyone agrees is 'bad luck', and you really believe that actual bad luck will follow, it means there has to be some form of agency, with a process in place. Go with me on this: if there's a process, then the various stages need to be thought through.

To save you the bother, I have thought them through for you. You can thank me later.

Firstly there has to be an observer, presumably with a clipboard (or nowadays a tablet), who is able to monitor all our actions, all the time, and can see each and every possible breach of a bad luck superstition. Put new shoes on the table? Walked under a ladder? Aha! Spotted you! Gotcha!

Then there needs to be an interpretive stage, where the observer can clearly determine that an infraction has taken place. Did Jonathan genuinely believe it was Twelfth Night when he took his decorations down, even though he was in fact a day late? Or did he walk under that ladder because to go around it would have meant stepping into the road and being knocked down by a passing car? Or maybe he saw a single magpie, but happened to be distracted by it and didn't spot the second one flying past?

Which then begs the question, is there a right of appeal? "I am sorry, M'lud, but I tripped and fell into the mirror; I did not mean to break it deliberately." Or is it the superstitious equivalent of a law of 'strict liability', where it's enough that the thing happened, and no intent needs to be proved?

Let's assume it is. Then, once a breach has been observed and verified, there needs to be some means of delivering the consequential dose of bad luck. A sort of cosmic 'Bad Luck Genie', able to make the appropriate amount of shit hit the fan.

Of course, there are those who would say all this sounds like the work for a god (or God, if you're so inclined). Although it does seem an awful lot of work, given he's probably run off his feet catching up with all the thoughts and prayers sent his way by people who've seen a natural disaster on the news, or mislaid their car keys.

But there's a good reason why it can't be God. That's because apparently he has a plan. One which he delivers in his own mysterious way. So it doesn't seem likely that he can get side-tracked by people breaking superstitions and needing to be punished with the necessary dose of 'bad luck'. Especially as both the breach of the superstition and the misfortune that follows would necessarily be part of his plan anyway. Who needs free will, when you have God?

Or maybe our current God leaves this sort of thing to his Greek colleagues, who seemed way less deterministic and much more capricious. If so, then this would mean that if you believe in superstitions, then you also believe in Zeus and co – which does rather put you at odds with the modern religions. Think about it – Zeus dishing out a dose of bad luck because a Christian took his Christmas decorations down a day late? Nah – doesn't work, does it?

And finally, there's the whole attribution thing. What particular piece of bad luck occurred as a consequence of breaking the superstition? I mean, is it just a case of 'shit happens', or is there a direct cause-and-effect thing going on?

So, there we are. We have superstitions handed down like malevolent memes that threaten 'bad luck' if you break them, with no real explanation as to how the consequential 'bad luck' actually happens.

You couldn't make it up.

# Fourteen - Our toxic legacy

Or are we just toying with the environment?

16th January 2023

I happened to see a very depressing sight on my walk into the city recently, so I thought I would share it with you. Go with me on this; I happen to be in a sharing, caring kind of mood right now.

It was a black wheelie bin that had fallen over outside some houses and the contents were spilling out. What were those contents? A plastic child's toy of a garage, complete with bright red ramps and parking bays. The kind of thing that is designed for kids to play with by driving their toy cars in and out, accompanied by 'brrrmmm brrrmmm' noises. It looked in pretty good condition to me as I walked past – as if there was nothing actually wrong with it. Yet it had been discarded, for whatever reason, into the refuse (landfill) bin. Not even the recycling bin, for what that's worth. Now I do understand, there may have been many reasons why it had been thrown out like this, and I accept that without knowing what the real one was, I was simply a passer-by who was jumping to a conclusion. But as I say, go with me on this; the conclusion I jumped to was one that I found very depressing.

And what was that conclusion? It was that a perfectly good toy had been thrown away to landfill – which symbolised the way we have become such a throwaway consumer society. Particularly with toys after Christmas. And why was that depressing? Because it shows just how damaging our actions are for the environment, and how badly we are cocking things up for future generations.

I know I am not saying anything new here (when do I ever?), but what that sight demonstrated to me was the madness of the consumer model when it comes to playthings for kids. Think about it. We import cheap plastic toys from China to give to our children, who play with them for a short while, until they get bored (or the batteries run out), then the item gets put in a cupboard and forgotten. Until eventually, sooner or later, it gets thrown into the wheelie bin, to be taken to landfill. Where it will fester un-decomposed, for generation after generation. And when it does finally decompose, I presume it will release billions of micro-plastic particles into the soil / atmosphere / oceans – all of which will seriously bugger up the environment and the biodiversity of the planet.

What possible excuse could we give to the future generations whose lives and environment we are blighting by the mountains of such plastic toys (not to mention the oceans of microplastics and wrappers we are bequeathing to the fish)? How can we possibly justify to them that what we were doing has any validity?

Imagine what we would say if a 'future generations person' popped back through a time-portal to find out what the heck is going on.

"You make millions of plastic toys," she says, "which you ship half way round the world (poisoning the atmosphere right there), put in colourful boxes and advertise on TV, so the kids pester their parents (or a made-up character in a red suit), to buy them for Christmas. Sooner or later the toy is discarded, to be buried in landfill under thousands of other such items, where it stays for hundreds or thousands of years like an environmental time-bomb, until we come along and have to deal with it. It sounds pretty dumb to me."

"No listen," we reply, "it's actually a really good idea. Not only do we get to see happy little faces on Christmas morning as they tear off the wrapping, but it also helps give us this amazing thing called 'economic growth', which means there's more and more money in the system."

"So everyone can buy more and more throwaway goods?"

"Well, not everyone – there are lots of people who can't afford to heat their homes or buy food, but that's another topic for another time.... Anyway, it's important we keep the economy growing, and making plastic toys is just one of the millions of ways we can do this."

"And the environment is just an unfortunate collateral victim," she observes.

"Absolutely. What's your problem with that?"

"The fact that we now have to deal with your mountain of toxic plastic waste."

"But," we say, "you can do so in the happy knowledge that not only did it keep our kids amused for a short while, it was also a vital part of our constant drive for economic growth."

I think we can all imagine what her response will be to that.

# Fifteen - We're hiring!

13th March 2023

We at 5 Minute Break have never shied away from jumping on a passing bandwagon. So, in view of the current need to avoid offending anyone, and the trend towards revising classic literature to fit with today's modern sensibilities, we have decided we need to appoint a **Head of Sensitivities** to review our articles and highlight any content that might cause offence.

We recognise it's going to be quite a tough gig, as causing offence is written into the 5 Minute Break DNA like 'Brighton' through a stick of rock, but we definitely need to move with the times. So if you're interested in joining the team, please turn over for the full Job Description.

# JOB DESCRIPTION

**Role:**
Head of Sensitivities

**Organisation:**
5 Minute Break

**Background:**
There are many things in today's world that don't seem to make any sense. Pedestrians who scatter others in the streets because they're staring at their phones while walking, those who make their lips look like sink-plungers and people who still believe in bronze-age mythologies – all of these, and more, leave us feeling bemused, confused, and quite frankly, nonplussed.

In response to this, 5 Minute Break was set up as a blog – in the hope that by sharing our confusion, we might help fellow-sufferers get a glimmer of understanding into what the heck is going on. Or at least, have a laugh. We put out what we believe are amusing, challenging or downright offensive articles, highlighting some particularly confusing element of modern life.

But as the song says, 'the times they are a-changing'. Nowadays you are not allowed to cause offence to anyone. Even books like Roald Dahl, James Bond and Ladybird are being revised. Sod the historical context – it's the offence (real or perceived) that counts.

So we're jumping on the bandwagon, and setting ourselves the goal of making 5 Minute Break as inoffensive as possible – and to make this happen, we're hiring a **Head of Sensitivities**.

**Scope of the Role:**
To read each article prior to publication, and to remove any or all elements that might just possibly cause the teensiest bit of offence to someone, or anyone. Whether or not it actually does.

**The ideal candidate:**
As **Head of Sensitivities** you will be supremely self-confident and totally aligned with all the '-isms' doing the rounds – and be able to spot inappropriate language at thirty paces. You will understand what might cause offence in others, be they men, women or somewhere in-between. You will combine both empathy and condescension; there's no minority – physical, mental or social – that you can't identify with. And be deeply offended on their behalf. Your supreme self-confidence will enable you to justify your revisionism on the basis of the current sensibilities rather than historical context, although you are prepared to change your views in accordance with the latest trends on X (aka Twitter). You will also have a thick skin (please accept our sincerest apologies if you are thick-skinist) – and will therefore be flexible and understanding if some, or all, of your changes are completely ignored. As they will be. Every time.

**Role and responsibilities:**
As the 5 Minute Break **Head of Sensitivities** you will be expected to keep on top of all the latest issues on all the social media platforms, and be able to assume any offence that could possibly be taken. You will also be expected to have a good knowledge of all the major world religions, and advise on which ones are least likely to take offence in response to any article we may write.

**Location:**
Working from home is encouraged, mainly as we don't actually have an office.

**Benefits:**
Flexible hours, allowing for time to review each article, and time to attend a zoom call discussion on why your changes won't actually be actioned.
Unlimited teas, coffees and snacks (which you will provide for your own consumption in your own home. No expenses).
Bring your pet to work. If you have one.

**Remuneration:**
Are you kidding? This is an opportunity to showcase your creativity and build your profile.

**Application process and timing:**
Applications must be submitted by email before the cut-off date (now closed). All first-round applicants will be required to demonstrate their suitability by submitting proposed revisions to an existing 5 Minute Break article. Candidates who are able to produce a revised version of any article that doesn't cause any offence at all, yet still actually makes sense, will be prioritised for a second-round interview, ideally in a local pub. Mine's a lager.

**Social Responsibility:**
5 Minute Break is an equal opportunities employer. We have to say that, apparently.

Thank you. Good luck to all applicants.

# Sixteen - Be more… meh!

How does that work?

4th July 2022

After a career in marketing, and now as a full-time author/publisher, I take a keen interest in how people and companies communicate with eachother. I have always believed in the principle of *KIS – keep it simple*. If you ask people to grasp multiple messages at the same time, you are likely to risk confusion – so best to communicate a single message, clearly and simply.

Which is all very well – but I think there's another principle which is becoming increasingly important in today's world of global communications, where it's hard to know what's real and what's fake, and where every crackpot opinion can be aired.

This principle is '*make everything honest*,' or *MEH* for short.

Let me give you some examples where the correct response to communications is *meh!* But first a bit of context. I am not talking about the eye-poppingly, jaw-droppingly, recklessly arrogant fake-newsery that we get from the world's so-called leaders. The kind of dishonesty that is so brazen that it challenges you to believe it because it is *so* unbelievable. You know the kind of thing;

…it wasn't a party it was a works do…

…it's a special military operation…

…I actually won the election…

No, what I'm talking about is the lower-level everyday communications we encounter as we go about our lives, where some Orwellian doublespeak has made its way through the corporate approval process and strides arrogantly into our lives like a school bully rolling up its sleeves and daring us to fight.

Let's start with some obvious candidates:

…your call is important to us… (if it was that important they would answer it quicker)

…we're experiencing a higher number of calls than usual… (this is a standard message – so when are you ever experiencing a lower number?)

…we record all calls for training purposes… (or so they've got you if you query them later)

…please gamble responsibly… (we have to say that so it's not our fault if you don't)

…click here to confirm you have read and understood the terms and conditions… (we know you haven't read them, let alone understood them. But if it ever came to court, our arses are covered).

Those are the doublespeak ones. There are also some where the communication is just plain inaccurate.

The first is the automatic message that pops up on my computer when I search for something. It says 'we' are responding. '*WE*'? It's a machine, for goodness sake! I know the programmers are trying to make it sound all chummy and human, but I do KNOW it's a machine! It's not like there's some remote team of software employees who have seamlessly taken over the workings of my laptop without me being aware (goodness, I hope not!) Or maybe a load of little guys inside, running around pulling levers and looking in files (although that could be an interesting idea to pitch to Disney Pixar).

So please, computer – don't tell me that 'we' couldn't find an answer to my search – use the *meh* principle and tell me that 'the programme could not find an answer.' Or if you want to be passive aggressive, 'an answer could not be found.' At least it doesn't then suggest you 'have a nice day'. Then my blood really would boil.

The next is when the motorway dot matrix signs tell you there's a hazard ahead and you need to slow down. Now I am as safety-conscious as the next guy, but I firmly believe that these signs are actually the CAUSE of motorway problems, not the solution. That's because they tell you to go slow for maybe 5-10 miles before the possible obstruction, which is almost NEVER actually there. So if you were to follow the instructions and go at 40mph or 30mph as the signs say for 10 miles, you would be an absolute menace, causing other traffic to brake sharply or swerve around you. And as I say, nine times out of ten, there's no actual obstruction ahead. I suspect it's because these signs adopt a massively over-cautious approach and operate on the basis of 'better safe than sorry' – when perhaps they should operate on more of a *meh* principle.

Here's a thought. If Google Maps can pinpoint a traffic jam down to a few metres, surely these dot-matrix signs can be made to be more accurate? More *meh*?

My final non-*meh* communication is train arrival times. We've all been there – waiting on the platform and looking at the times of our train on the overhead signs. Let's suppose the expected arrival time comes up as an on-schedule 08:41. Then a few minutes later, it flickers and changes to 08:50. And a few minutes later, it flickers again and becomes 08:59. And so on… you get the idea.

So this begs the question – at what point did they know the actual train arrival time? Surely they can work out where it is now, the average speed of the track in front of it and the number of stops – to give a fairly accurate assessment of its arrival time? It's not as if the average speed on a certain part of the track suddenly changes – like on a road when Bert and Doris in their Austin 1100 unexpectedly pull out in front of you, then pootle along at 30mph (no doubt they're obeying a dot matrix sign). Could the people who run the train signage not be a bit more *meh*, and stop giving a series of 'hoped-for' times, and give one accurate one instead?

Or maybe it's the computers they use? If the accuracy of their computer's data download status bar is anything like mine, the expected completion time changes so often that it is wholly meaningless. So maybe the calculations of the train times are governed by the variable speed of the computers downloading the data?

'We are calculating the time of the train… Unfortunately we have not been able to calculate it to any level of accuracy. Have a nice day.'

*MEH!*

# Seventeen - Time, and sales, wait for no-one.

The god of consumerism needs his sacrifices.

8th August 2022

This time of the year I feel particularly sorry for school kids.

Why? Because this is the time when they break up for the summer, and just as they are enjoying the start of a few weeks where they don't have to think about school, the high street and out-of-town retailers have a different idea. "Oh no," they say, "your end of term coincides exactly with the start of our pre-season run-up for sales of new school uniforms and pencil cases." So when the kids set out for their first foray down the high street, (which they seem to do a lot, in fairly large groups), they are confronted with shop windows screaming BACK TO SCHOOL! It may just be me, but I can't believe that's a particularly welcome sight for them. It does rather make you wonder if the stores could be a bit more sensitive? Presumably parents are not going to buy new uniforms the moment the little darlings are out of school – I would have thought they would leave that sort of thing till the last minute, in case the little darlings are slightly bigger little darlings when term does start. So here's a thought, retailers – be a bit more understanding and leave the BACK TO SCHOOL! shop windows until maybe 1 or 2 weeks before the term restarts? Just a thought.

Of course, this pales into insignificance against the pre-selling bonanza that is Christmas. As you can probably imagine, I am not a fan of Christmas decorations being prominently on sale in the early autumn. It seems to me to be perverse that while we are still in summer mode, sweltering through the shops in shorts and t-shirts, we are confronted with snow-scenes, jolly red-suited and white-bearded mannequins and miles of tinsel. Do the stores really think we'll be inspired to start stocking up on baubles and wrapping paper before Strictly has even started? Perhaps Christmas displays could be embargoed before – I don't know – early December? Again – just a thought.

Both these are, to me, examples of the total dominance of consumerism in our modern western society. As we have become increasingly secular (a good thing though that may be), we have shifted our focus and are now worshiping at the high alter of retail. Instead of receiving the Host (which has always struck me as weird - are we supposed to be cannibals?) we offer up our own symbolic token, the credit card. We then solemnly pass this across the Holy Card Reader in order to affirm our total subservience to the god of Consumerism.

And it's not just the symbolism of religion that is transferring across to retailing, like the liquid metal in Terminator 2 flowing across the floor and reforming itself into a new robot. No, it's also the pastoral side as well. Where once we were known to the vicar or priest by name, now we are known by name in retail instead. I am, of course, referring to that slightly sickening practice of being asked our name when we go into a certain coffee shop, so they can spell it wrong on the cup and shout it out when your overpriced froth is ready (OK that was a cheap shot – I am actually quite partial to a cappuccino). I always mean to give them a stupid made-up name to protest against this awful American over-familiarity, but my nerve goes and I mutter 'Jonathan' when asked.

Then there's the checkout staff in my local supermarket, who have their names prominently displayed on badges, and have been told – no doubt by some memo from Management – that they have to strike up a cheery conversation with each customer. This is while the customer is struggling to pack their purchases into a bag faster than they come shooting down the conveyor like they were part of the Generation Game. It's clearly an attempt to create a 'relationship' – and in my opinion, toe-curlingly embarrassing for both parties. That sort of thing might work Stateside, but here in the UK we are a tad more reserved. So in the unlikely event that I do feel the sudden urge to be cheery and personal, I feel it's up to me to read their name badge and initiate the conversation. Although to be fair, that would probably be just as toe-curling as if they started it.

I even got an email from my energy supplier the other day, after a phone conversation about my bill. The email was signed 'Love & power, Joe' then a little emoji representing the company. This is a chap who didn't even know I existed until that morning, yet now he's sending emails signed like we've been best mates for years?

How terribly un-British.

# Eighteen - My life in my hands?

I'd better check.

26th September 2022

I'm sitting on a bus as I write this on my iPhone.

As a phone user, I see that I am among the majority on this bus; everyone else around me seems to have their heads bowed down to worship at the altar of their little screen. Fascinating countryside flashes by unnoticed (actually a suburban built-up road, but you get the idea), as everyone checks their socials, bashes out a text, krushes kandy (or whatever the latest inane game is now), or as in my case, writes their weekly blog.

And it's not just the bus. On my way to the stop, I walked up a line of slow-moving traffic, and if I was a policeman looking to meet my monthly target for nicking motorists using their mobiles at the wheel - I would have smashed it in a few minutes.

I have written at length about how much I dislike those who

walk along a crowded street with their nose buried in the screen, scattering responsible citizens like an ice-breaker ploughing through the Antarctic seas (see Chapter One), but it has dawned on me that walking and driving while looking at a mobile are just the tip of the iceberg. Whenever we have a single moment of inactivity, wherever we are, out comes the phone.

Settled into your cinema seat and the ads are still running? Check your emails (but then switch the bloody thing off for the film, unless of course, you want to be thought of as an inconsiderate moron).

Sitting down in a coffee shop for a 15 minute break in the day? Pass the time scrolling through your socials.

In a restaurant with friends and the conversation flags for a millisecond? Whip out your phone and check the stats on your latest tweet.

Actually the restaurant example above is not a good one. That's because we now have to use our mobiles to order food at the table, as many restaurants have maintained the pandemic practice of making you scan a QR code to bring up the menu, then order and pay by phone. I don't know whether to be pleased they're saving trees by not printing a menu, or upset they are forcing us to bury our noses in our screens like ostriches as soon as we sit down. On balance I suppose the environmental benefit trumps the anti-social screen-staring.

But I do have a confession here. For all I chunter on about the inconsiderate and anti-social use of phones, I do have to admit that I am actually something of a phone addict myself.

There, I have said it.

I check my Amazon book sales several times a day, looking for that dopamine hit when the little orange bar chart goes up.

If I see one of those little red circles that says I have mail, or a comment on my Instagram, I have to tap on it immediately, in case it's urgent.

And I love it when I take a peek at my Amazon or Goodreads

pages and find a new rating or review on one of my books.

Yes, I have to say it. I, too, am a phone addict.

I suppose it's inevitable that a single device with so many life-managing / enhancing functions becomes such an integral part of your life. It's a wonder we ever put it down at all.

Indeed, so much of my life is intertwined with the thing, that I would probably be a gibbering wreck if it was ever forcibly removed. Maybe I should go to one of those addiction meetings – I'm sure there's one for people who can't be parted from their phones…

"Good evening. Do sit down. You're new to our group?" says the severe-looking woman with the 1950s glasses and the tweed skirt as I walk nervously in.

I take a seat in the circle. "Yes. My name is Jonathan and… (I gulp, take a breath, then clear my throat) …I am a phone addict."

"I am pleased to hear you admit it," she replies. Then she holds out her hand with a raised eyebrow. "Give it to me," she says, with a look in her eye that makes me think of Medusa on a bad day.

I pull my phone out of my pocket, but don't hand it over. I can feel the prickling of sweat on my brow and the pounding of my heart, as she brings her hand ever closer. Then, just as I am about to clutch it to my chest like a parent protecting their child, her hand shoots out like a lizard's tongue and wraps around my phone. There's a nasty moment where it looks as if there's going to be a tussle, then I catch the gimlet eye behind her glasses, and I let go.

"Good. That is step one," she says, as she switches it off and puts it on her desk. "You can be without your phone for the next hour." She pauses. "An hour today. Then work your way up to two hours, and on to a daily routine where it only comes out for a few minutes at a couple of set times each day."

I nod weakly, not sure how I'll survive.

# Part 2

# Go with me on world events...

# Nineteen - God Save the Queen

From what?

June 6th 2022

*The UK had just celebrated the Queen's Platinum Jubilee, which began with a sketch of the Queen having tea with Paddington Bear.*

Now the dust has settled on the celebrations of the Queen's remarkable achievement in reaching 70 years on the throne, perhaps we can reflect on the words of the National Anthem which we heard played and sung so joyfully at the concert and other events over the weekend?

*God save our gracious Queen!*
*Long live our noble Queen!*

*God save the Queen!*
*Send her victorious,*
*Happy and glorious,*
*Long to reign over us,*
*God save the Queen.*

Have you ever considered what the words say, let alone what they mean? Have you wondered for example, what it is we are exhorting God to 'save' the Queen from? Or whether we should continue to ask that she should be 'long-lived?'

If so, perhaps a perfectly valid response from God might be that as the lady in question has reached the impressive age of 96, which part of 'saving' her and giving her a long life, do we think he has missed? Surely, he might argue, he can put a big tick in the 'saving' box, and we should perhaps now be moving on and asking him for something else in regard to this exceptional person?

Of course, all this is academic, if you take the more theological view that what we're actually doing is asking God to be a Christian 'saviour'; in other words, to 'save' the Queen in the same way that Jesus was supposed to be sent to save all of us – from 'original sin'. This was the sin derived from the actions of Adam, Eve and the Serpent, involving a certain apple in the Garden of Eden, as told in the book of Genesis. Unless you are a committed creationist and believe that the earth is only 6,000 years old, it was created in six days and that snakes can talk – in which case you are probably part of a very small minority in Britain today – this is hardly a valid request.

Either way, by asking God to save Her Majesty from death, or from 'original sin', I think this makes the National Anthem into a form of prayer. Great Britain is now a diverse and multicultural society, and although 54.7% of the 2011 census respondents described themselves as Christian, 35.3% described themselves as having no religion. And I suspect that these figures will have shifted significantly further away from Christianity when the 2021 census figures are released later this year (*editor's note: They did. Big time*).

I would therefore argue that this makes the words of the anthem – which dates back to 1745 – singularly inappropriate to modern Britain. Surely we should have a National Anthem that better reflects our society and beliefs today? I suggest when the sadly inevitable does happen and we have to bid a fond and heartfelt farewell to Her Majesty, that the new King Charles should use his influence to start a national debate on our anthem.

Should it have any exhortation to God at all? I accept that Charles will be head of the established church, but surely it is inappropriate for the song we sing at national events to be so deeply based on a religion that fewer and fewer of us subscribe to, or even believe in? Another anomaly is that the National Anthem is British, while there is no equivalent anthem (to the best of my knowledge) for the English. The Welsh have *Hen Wlad Fy Nhadau* and the Scots have *Flower of Scotland* – yet as part of the United Kingdom, both also have *God Save the Queen*. This leads to the interesting spectacle that when either of these teams play England at an international rugby match they each sing their own anthem, while the English team sings one that applies equally to both sides.

So let's have a national debate on the National Anthem – not now, as I say, but once God has stopped saving Queen Elizabeth – and find something more appropriate to modern Britain, and maybe also a different one for modern England. Naturally, I would rather this is later than sooner, not least because it would be great for God save our current sovereign for as long as possible, but also because she has revealed herself to be a fine comedy actress. No matter how old she is, it was clear on Saturday night that she has impeccable timing, and can deliver a comedy punchline with the best of them.

More tea with Paddington Bear, anyone?

# Twenty - Remembering Queen Elizabeth II

1926-2022

12th September 2022

*Sadly, only three months after the Platinum Jubilee, Queen Elizabeth II passed away.*

In view of the very sad news from last Thursday and out of respect for Her Majesty, my usual 'cynical old codger' rant about modern life has been put on hold for this week.

Instead I just want to pay tribute to this remarkable lady, who maintained not only a strong sense of dignity and duty, but also managed to keep her sense of humour throughout the longest reign in our nation's history.

Whatever you may think about her embodiment of wealth and elitist privilege (something I believe you will always have, whatever system of government is in power) I would make two points:

She didn't choose her position – she was born into it. Sure, she could have walked away, but she didn't. She decided to play the hand that life had dealt her with an amazing dedication to duty and with a remarkable sense of personal integrity.

She remained above politics, serving as an impartial Head of State, providing a source of stability and wisdom to all our political leaders for over 70 years.

One particular story from 1998 resonates most for me, showing how she was prepared to use her soft power to make a very firm point. For this I am indebted to Huffpost, and am quoting from their 2015 story by Dominique Mosbergen. My amends [in brackets] are for clarity and to reflect changes since the article was written.

The story was excerpted in The Sunday Times from a memoir by British diplomat Sir Sherard Cowper-Coles, who was appointed Ambassador to Saudi Arabia in 2003. It begins with Abdullah [bin Abdulaziz] – then the crown prince and de facto ruler of Saudi Arabia – visiting Balmoral.

'After lunch, the Queen had asked her royal guest whether he would like a tour of the estate,' wrote Cowper-Coles, who is said to have heard the tale from both Elizabeth and Abdullah themselves. 'Prompted by his foreign minister the urbane Prince Saud, an initially hesitant Abdullah had agreed. The royal Land Rovers were drawn up in front of the castle. As instructed, the Crown Prince climbed into the front seat of the front Land Rover, his interpreter in the seat behind.'

Little did Abdullah know, however, that his driver for the day would be none other than Elizabeth herself.

'To his surprise, the Queen climbed into the driving seat, turned the ignition and drove off,' Cowper-Coles wrote.

‘Women [were not at that time] allowed to drive in Saudi Arabia, and Abdullah was not used to being driven by a woman, let alone a queen.’

Not to mention a queen who [could] drive like the wind. According to Cowper-Coles, Elizabeth didn’t just drive the SUV, but rapidly whizzed along the estate’s roads as she chatted, prompting Abdullah to become increasingly anxious.

‘Through his interpreter, the Crown Prince implored the Queen to slow down and concentrate on the road ahead,’ the diplomat said.

Saudi Arabia was at the time the only country in the world that forbade women from driving. The Queen showed the Crown Prince, in her own way and with a wicked sense of humour, how wrong and out of touch this policy was. And in 2018 the ban on women driving was lifted in Saudi Arabia. Wouldn’t it be nice to think that our Queen was, in part, responsible?

So I can only conclude with the words I wrote in the Book of Condolence:

Goodbye Ma’am. And thank you.

# Twenty-one - A period of the dullest TV

Is that what she would have wanted?

20th September 2022

*After the Queen's coffin had been driven to Westminster for the lying-in-state, the public were allowed to file past and pay their respects.*

**Scene**

*Westminster Hall, London, the day before the funeral.*
*A TV Reporter and Cameraman advance on tearful woman.*
*The Reporter waves a microphone in her face.*

**Reporter** Good afternoon, madam. Can I just stop you here, and ask how long you were queuing to see Her Majesty?

**Woman** Only 11 hours. The queue moved very quickly.

**Reporter** And may I ask where are you from?

**Woman** Dudley

**Reporter** Gosh, that's a long way to come.

**Woman** I just felt I had to travel down here and see her. (*Wipes away tear*). Or at least, see a coffin under a flag with a crown on top.

**Reporter** And is this the first time you've seen her?

**Woman** Oh no. She once smiled at me from her car window. She was so gracious. I felt personally blessed.

**Reporter** Lovely. And where was that?

**Woman** I think it was when she was in Jamaica.

**Reporter** Oh wow! Were you there on holiday?

**Woman** Oh no, I was in Dudley.

**Reporter** (*After a pause*) You mean – it was when you saw her on the telly?

**Woman** Oh yes. She looked straight at me. It was such a precious moment. I will remember it for the rest of my life.

**Reporter** (*Smiles weakly*). I think we'll end it there. Thank you madam. (*Turns to camera*). So, as you can see, everyone has their special story about the Queen to tell – she touched so many lives. (*Spots a man with dark glasses and a guide dog*). Excuse me, sir, can we have a word?

**Dog** Yes, no problem.

**Reporter** I beg your pardon?

**Dog** Sure. Happy to talk. (*Looks up at camera*). Is this live? I have always wanted to be on the TV.

**Reporter** I… er… Yes… Right. Can you, or your… er… master… tell us why you wanted to see the Queen today?

**Dog** I always felt she was my queen, you know what I mean? I realise she was into corgis and all that, but one could see she was really a queen for all breeds. All dogs. (*Pause*). Although not mongrels, obviously. (*Laughs*).

**Reporter** Er… yes... I mean, no… Can you tell me what it was like to see her today?

**Dog** Very moving. I had to bow my head as we passed. (*Wipes away tear with paw*).

**Reporter** And your master..?

**Dog** I'm sure he was equally moved.

**Reporter** (*To the man*) Can you not tell me yourself, sir?

**Dog** I doubt it. I do everything for him. Cook, clean, talk…

**Reporter** That's very good of you. So what does he do all day?

**Dog** He rehearses his act.

**Reporter** Oh, is he a performer? (*Dog nods and wags tail*). What does he perform?

**Dog** He's a ventriloquist. (*The dog winks, then leads the man away*).

**Reporter** (*After a few moments, takes a deep breath and walks up to a mum and young daughter*). Ah, madam. And your daughter? How nice to see you here. Can you tell our viewers what it has been like for you today?

**Mum** It's been wonderful.

**Reporter** She's been the queen all your life. Will you miss her?

**Mum** (*Wipes away tear*). Oh yes.

**Reporter** (*Waves microphone under daughter's nose*). It must have been a long day for you. How old are you?

**Daughter** I'm seven.

**Reporter** Lovely. So you finally got to see the Queen?

**Daughter** Sort of. Or a coffin under a flag with a crown on top.

**Reporter** I see, yes. And was it like losing your nan?

**Daughter** Not necessarily.

**Reporter** Why is that?

**Daughter** As you ask, she was not like my nan, she was the monarch and she was head of the church. I think that makes the monarchy an anachronism in Britain of the 21st century. There's no justification for an established church when fifty-three percent of the population describe themselves as 'non-faith'. I trust the new King Charles, who has said he wants to be a 'defender of faiths' rather than 'defender of THE faith,' recognises that the largest faith group is those who don't have one. And not only that, but faiths other than C of E make up a significant proportion of those that do believe. I think this makes his position as Supreme Governor of the Church of England increasingly tenuous. I hope he therefore moves towards disestablishment as a matter of priority.

**Reporter** Right… (*Sighs*). Right… Thank you… (*As the mum and daughter wander off, he turns to the Cameraman*). Stop rolling will you? You stopped? We're off air? (*The Cameraman nods and looks out from the eyepiece*). All the other networks get boring people chuntering on about how great she was, and how they shook hands with her in 2003, and how it was like losing their nan. That's how it's supposed to be; the most boring TV ever. Wallpaper telly. In keeping with the solemnity of the occasion. You know – the monarch dies and while the radio plays sombre music, the TV shows nothing but three hours of a hearse driving through the countryside followed by 100-plus hours of people walking past the coffin. Boring. Predictable. Dull. It's what we prepared for – people trotting out the expected banalities on vox pop interviews to reporters wearing black ties, like they're reading out social media memes on a loop. That's what's expected. That's what proper telly should be until after the funeral. (*Sighs*). Ah well. Let's try that man over there. The one with the glasses and nasal hair. Maybe he'll be OK…

# Twenty-two - Why do we have a Coronation?

It's not what you might think.

8th May 2023

*The coronation of King Charles III and Queen Camilla took place at Westminster Abbey on 6th May 2023.*

Ahh, the King's Coronation. Pomp, ceremony, tradition and, of course, lashings of rain. Did it make you proud to be British? Or if you're not from this Kingdom, did it make you wish you were?

It might surprise you, but in this article I am not going to use the Coronation as an excuse to take a swipe at the monarchy or the King; crusty old cynic that I am. No, instead I am going to use it to ask the question 'why do we have a Coronation?'

But more of that shortly. Firstly I want to say that watching it confirmed to me that I am actually in favour of a hereditary monarchy. It made me realise that there is a very strong justification for Charles becoming head of state – a position that stands above politics – purely by virtue of being the firstborn son of the late Queen.

You don't agree? Think of the alternative. If you select a head of state by vote, you get opposing candidates – and what does that bring with it? Yup. Political parties. Which means you get political manifestos promising what each candidate would do if voted into office, and you have a victor who represents only those who voted for them – almost certainly less than half the population. And a manifesto, for all the promises it makes, cannot realistically be implemented by a constitutional figurehead who has no political power. Which makes it pointless.

Contrast that with selection by heredity. A system that gives us a King or Queen, who, whatever you might think of them, stands above politics and is therefore able to represent the whole population.

But if you still want elections, I would ask you this. Who would you get as candidates? Ex-politicians or faded 'celebs' who are unlikely to have the stature of a head of state, nor any real political neutrality. I'm sorry, but I don't think these are people I want representing my country on the world stage. (What's that? President Zelensky is an ex-comedian? I know – there are exceptions to every rule). But exceptions aside, give me a man who's spent 60+ years being prepared for the role over someone like, I don't know – Blair, Cameron or Johnson.

So, I am not using this article to have a go at the King, nor at the monarchy as an institution. They may not be perfect, but in my humble opinion, they're a whole heap better than the alternative.

No, my question is, why do we need a Coronation ceremony at all?

I watched the service in Westminster Abbey with that thought uppermost in my mind.

And if you watched it with unquestioning acceptance, then I want to answer the above question with the following answer - that we neither need, nor should have, such a ceremony.

Because what I saw was a sickening display of arrogance and anachronism by the established Anglican Church.

I'm sorry if you're a committed Anglican, but there is absolutely no place for an established religion in today's Britain, and certainly not for that religion to validate the monarch. Here's an interesting statistic – apparently less than 1% of the population attend weekly Anglican services (2021 Census). Let me put that another way: an institution that 99% of us do not regularly support claims the authority to install our head of state.

And it's not as if the coronation is even necessary. Under the 1701 Act of Settlement, the Prince of Wales became King Charles the moment his mother passed away. The Coronation serves only one official purpose; to install him as the head of the established Anglican church. The 'defender of the faith' even. So, to spend £250m of tax-payer money on a ceremony that has little or no relevance to 99% of the tax-paying population is, quite frankly, indefensible.

And boy, didn't the church elite seem to love their moment in the glare of the world's publicity? What a chance to grandstand their anachronistic and irrational practices! The church has said it sees the coronation as a "unique opportunity" to convert people to Christianity. *WHAT?* The church has used £250m of our money to proselytise to us? And it doesn't stop there. As part of the ceremony, the King was stripped down to his shirt, and consecrated with 'holy oil' behind a privacy screen. According to the Westminster Abbey website, "This sacred blessing… is at the heart of the Christian coronation service, demonstrating the connection between the monarch and God."

That'll be a 'god' that fewer and fewer of Charles's subjects actually believe in, then?

As I say, maybe you glossed over all this when you watched the ritual. Focussed on the pomp and ceremony. Revelled in the eyes of the world being on Britain for a day. Marvelled at us Brits putting on one heck of a show. And yes, you knew that there would be a load of 'Jesus'-ing, 'Oh Lord'-ing and 'Almighty God'-ing going on, but you let it wash over you, because you've heard it all many, many times before. After all, it's so familiar that the actual meaning no longer sinks in.

Well, I would like to challenge you with a few things that may have passed you by, but which jumped out at me as I watched.

Firstly, the sheer opulence and wealth on display. Not only the priceless jewels in the crowns and regalia, but all the gold – in the coaches, the vestments, the plates and the adornments of the abbey itself. Let me just remind you of the originator of this religion – a mythical Jewish carpenter who blessed the poor and the needy, and asked his followers to give up their worldly goods. A bloke who said that his so-called 'kingdom of heaven' was not open to the wealthy. Yeah, that mythical bloke. So when you see the amount of wealth concentrated into the hands of the church elite, it becomes quite clear that this religion was never really about moral philosophy – it was always just a means for the elite to control the rest of the population. That's why it needed to demonstrate its 'other-worldliness' to support its power with conspicuous wealth. But thankfully, Britain no longer seems to care. The increasing irrelevance of the church's levers of power – its promise of eternal 'bliss' in heaven and the threat of eternal 'torture' in hell – means that its power and control is slipping away like a receding tide. And in doing so, it reveals what it really is – a colourful, showy human organisation that has gathered massive wealth over the centuries, and seems to have no desire to relinquish it.

Secondly, the parade of bishops flocking around the King like purple and white crows. These are people who have a constitutional right to sit in the House of Lords, and therefore vote on legislation. Think about that a moment. Adults who have consciously left logic and rationality at the church door in favour of myth, superstition and proven falsehoods, and whose true constituency is less than 1% of the population, are able to vote on laws that affect the entire country. You only have to look across the pond to the anti-democratic theocrats in the USA to see how that can turn out.

And thirdly, the invocation to their 'god' for the authority to crown the King. Charles himself even undermined that, with his oath to serve, rather than be served. In other words, he was claiming his authority from the people, rather than specifically from any 'god'. Not that Welby and his fellow bishops seemed to spot the contradiction.

So, there it is. We have a new King as our head of state. All well and good. We just didn't need an expensive, irrelevant coronation, born out of ancient authoritarianism, to legitimise him. It demonstrates to me just how out of touch the Anglican church is, and the sooner it is disestablished, the better. Hopefully before the current Prince of Wales becomes King William V. We can then devise some secular way to signify the transfer of the crown when that time comes.

We should certainly recognise that Great Britain is no longer the 'god-fearing' society that the Anglican church seems to think it is.

Or wants to make it again.

# Part 3

# Go with me on religion...

# Twenty-three - The compelling case against religion

And why you should look on the bright side of life instead

28th November 2022

As you might have guessed from a few well-chosen throwaway remarks in previous articles, I make no secret of my disbelief in all things religious.

Let me see if I can quantify this for you. In The God Delusion Professor Richard Dawkins puts forward a 7-point scale of belief, where 1 is certainty that a god exists and 7 is certainty that none exists. I understand Professor Dawkins rates himself as a 6, saying, "I cannot know for certain but I think God is very improbable, and I live my life on the assumption that he is not there." I go one step further, and put myself firmly as a 7. Or maybe even a 7+. Everything I have seen and heard since my mid-teens has convinced me that the only logical unifying explanation for all the contradictory and unproven claims of religions over the past few thousand years is that they are man-made stories. In fact, I am convinced that the god of the old and new testaments is as fictional as the characters that I make up for my own novels. If a lot more cruel and genocidal than they are.

I mention that my atheism started in my mid-teens. Up till then I had been a 'light' Christian, broadly accepting and not particularly questioning the religious information that I had been fed. My parents had taken a very liberal view and not forced me into any religion at home, but had sent me to schools that were essentially Church of England. They had then neither confirmed nor denied what I heard in the school chapel services, but left me to make up my own mind.

Looking back, I don't think I particularly listened to those chapel services, other than to mentally 'tick off' that the key points were in place (Jesus loves me – check. Be nice to others – check. Christmas is coming with lots of gifts – yayy! Check).

Then one day when I was in school chapel I decided to actually listen to – and analyse – what the chaplain was saying. And it amazed me when I realised that what was coming from his mouth was utter bullshit! How had I not seen this before? It was a mixture of trite platitudes, vapid clichés and obvious untruths presented as fact. I wondered how I had ever believed in such rubbish. And as I recall, it seemed to me from the way he trotted it out that he didn't appear to believe in it either.

It was as if a bubble had burst. It was gone! Religion was no longer something I could – or would – accept.

I think it was shortly after this that I saw Monty Python's Life of Brian, a brilliant deconstruction of mindless faith which definitely cemented my atheism. I have since seen the TV debate John Cleese and Michael Palin had at the time with Malcolm Muggeridge and some bishop who seemed off-the-scale in pomposity.

If you haven't seen it, check it out on YouTube – you might find it very entertaining.

How John Cleese managed to keep his temper amazes me, and at one point it looks to me as if Michael Palin is prepared to sacrifice his 'nice guy' image and punch the bishop in the face. Personally I wouldn't have blamed him if he had - the old bloke certainly seemed to deserve it. One of his and Muggeridge's arguments was to suggest that if a fourteen-year-old boy saw this 'tenth-rate little film', what would it do to his faith? Well, I am here to tell you exactly what it would do – as I was that boy. It would demonstrate just how laughably man-made religion is, and how unworthy it is of any respect.

So here I am, all these years later, a committed unbeliever in religious twaddle, and a firm believer in the power of humanity to do good without the need for religion. I am always ready to champion the cause of rational secularism / humanism, and defend it robustly in an open-minded discussion with any theist. If it is possible to find a theist who is not too militant to have such a discussion.

Sadly it is often the theists who accuse atheists of being militant; trying to force their 'atheist beliefs' on others. What? Atheism is not a belief-system in its own right - but simply the lack of belief in the unsubstantiated claims of theists.

For me, the case against religions in general – and Christianity in particular – is very clear. Unlike Christianity, atheism does not actually seek to force any sort of creed on others:

- Atheism does not send out missionaries and armies to convert indigenous populations against their will.
- Atheism does not forcefully indoctrinate vulnerable children by filling their heads with nonsense – and particularly terrify them with the disproportionate threat of everlasting torture – when they are too young to distinguish fact from fiction.

- Atheism does not preach hate against out-group minorities, nor burn non-believers at the stake.
- Atheism does not claim to own morality, and especially not a morality that is derived from a religious book written by ignorant bronze-age goat-herders and therefore irrelevant to modern society.
- Atheism does not massively hinder human progress by closing its mind to proven science.
- Atheism does not demand money in return for the promise of a vague, unsubstantiated reward after death.
- Atheism does not champion the rights of an insentient clump of cells over the rights of a living, breathing, feeling woman.
- Atheism does not propagate AIDS or poverty by refusing to allow condoms, nor protect paedophiles who abuse children in their care.
- Atheism does not terrorise children with threats of an all-seeing, all-knowing, judgemental god who watches them 24/7 and even peers into their innermost thoughts.
- Atheism does not encourage a lack of personal responsibility by suggesting that all actions are the result of either divine or satanic will.
- Atheism does not suggest that by having conversations in your head with an imaginary friend, you can make change happen in the real world, or 'cleanse your sins'.
- Atheism does not send its followers out to kill those who believe in a different imaginary friend.
- And – atheism does not suggest that we all need to be 'saved' from the actions of a mythical talking snake and a woman created from a earth-man's rib.

No, atheism is not a belief system, and it does not force its philosophy on anyone. It simply presents the case for a rational secular life that is more progressive, more open, more inclusive and more rational than anything offered by religion.

Which is why I for one, will continue to make the case for atheism as much as I can.

Always look on the bright side of life, everyone!

# Twenty-four - An unholy f-bomb

Or how we learned to love the effing Word

18th July 2022

***WARNING: This article makes very liberal use of the f-word. If you are someone that finds this offensive, I suggest you stop reading now. If, however, you are offended by any views of religion that contradict your own, then I invite you to read on, but at your own risk.***

It seems to me that nothing better describes the move in modern free-thinking western societies from religion to secularism, than the substitution of the f-word for 'god' in the phrase 'for god's sake!'

Now I know what you're thinking. "For fuck's sake, Jonathan!" you say, "how can you build an argument for secularisation around one little phrase? There must be hundreds of other indicators, such as falling church attendance and fewer people claiming to have a religion or believe in god. Or even the marginalisation of the clergy in national debates. And yes, you are quite right, those indicators do suggest that religion is on the run in most, if not quite all, western societies (the 'Land of the Free?' Fuck, give me strength).

But go with me on this.

A very learned Roman philosopher called Seneca once observed a very, very long time ago, 'Religion is regarded by the common people as true, by the wise as false, and by rulers as useful.' Religion worked in bronze-age and early societies as primarily a means of social control. Its basic precept was that if you disobeyed 'god's law' – which by happy coincidence was virtually indistinguishable from the needs of the powerful elite – then you would go to hell. Indeed in biblical times their god seemed to think slavery and misogyny were perfectly acceptable, while eating shellfish or pork, uncovering your head, working on the Sabbath or wearing mixed fabrics were worthy of eternal torture in fire and brimstone. Fuck knows why.

One of the key commandments that this god felt was so imperative that he passed it on via his spokesman Moses (not in person of course, as that would mean showing himself), was not to take his name in vain. "Do that," he grumbled, "and you had better get measured up for an asbestos suit, and pronto."

But now it is seen as perfectly acceptable to not only take a god's name in vain, but to substitute it for 'fuck'; a word that represents the kind of sin that got the bronze-age elders so hot under the collar. To me, this casual everyday 'blasphemy' demonstrates that we no longer live in fear of divine retribution - and specifically the threat of being burned for all eternity by an ever-loving god when we die. If that threat is lifted, then it shows clearly that the power that religion once held as a means of social control is gone. Gone, but unfortunately not forgotten.

"Aha!" You might say, "but the point you are missing Jonathan, is that religion provides us with a basis for our morality. Without reference to a higher authority, how can we know what is right or wrong?"

But when it comes to the biblical morality of Christianity, (the only religion I can talk about with any confidence), that doesn't work for me. There are two reasons:

1. A person who says their morality comes from the bible must be ignoring all the verses (across both testaments) that condone genocide, rape, incest, slavery, torture, misogyny, family abandonment, cannibalism, sacrifice and threats of damnation. If they only focus on the 'god is love' message, then by what moral standards are they making such a choice? By definition it must be a higher level of morality than the bible itself - and presumably a similar morality practiced by those who do not believe in their god.
2. Doing good because you want to be rewarded in heaven (or not tortured in hell) is a morality based on self-interest not empathy. I think that a truer type of morality is when someone does good because they care deeply about their fellow living creatures and the natural environment. Not because they are trying to book their own ticket to heaven.

Of course, there are those who still believe their religion gives them *carte blanche* to impose their interpretation of morality upon all citizens, regardless of whether or not those other citizens happen to share their beliefs. Which is, of course, a perfect definition of social control by religion.

To which the only valid response is surely "For fuck's sake, keep your bronze-age morality to yourselves and let everyone else get on with their lives."

# Twenty-five - OMG! Please clarify

Which god is that exactly?

29th May 2023

Those of you who were regular *Friends* watchers from 1994 to 2004 – and the repeats ever since – will know how Janice (Maggie Wheeler) makes the iconic exclamation 'OH – MY – GOD!' in her trademark squeaky voice. And she's not the only one; I am sure most people say the same thing many times in the course of their daily lives. It, and the abbreviation 'OMG!', seem to be acceptable responses to any situation, from the mildly interesting to the slightly surprising, and all the way up to the truly unexpected.

But those of you who have read this far will know that I like to understand the meaning behind such expressions and 'unpack' them (OMG! I so hate that expression). It seems to me that the question here is this – when you say, 'Oh my god!' which particular god are you appealing to? In the context of the question, which god is yours?

It could be any one of the three or four thousand gods that human societies have worshipped, ever since man first stepped out of his cave and knelt down before the sun to pray it would come back again the next day. Is it Yahweh, Jesus, Allah or Vishnu perhaps? Or maybe it's Zeus, Odin, Apollo or Thor? Then again, could it be Isis, Horus, Anubis or Osiris? Or could it even be a personal god; one that you have in your head that no-one else knows about? While I am not going to pry into which god you are claiming to own, it would be interesting to know which it is.

That's because different gods might be expected to react to your invocation in different ways. Say you see a social post from a friend, showing how they are relaxing on a sunny beach, while you are shivering into your anorak on your rainy commute. 'OH – MY – GOD!' you exclaim as you stare at the pictures of them relaxing on a beach lounger, holding up their daquiri like a prize trophy and grinning like a Cheshire cat. If Jesus is your particular god, he might be expected to observe that envy is not a good look on you, then add something about the meek inheriting the earth, before then taking no further action (which seems to be his way). But if say, Thor is your go-to god, he might be more inclined to offer a thunderbolt delivery service, and take the friend out with a quick blast of lightning, which would emerge inexplicably from the cloudless sky over Tenerife. You get the point – different gods work in different ways (all of them mysterious).

Then again, what if you say 'OMG!', but don't happen to believe in any god at all? Are you being disingenuous by appealing to 'your' god when you don't actually have one? Or is it that the expression has lost all meaning in this modern age, where so much of the western world is becoming secular? Do committed atheists also throw 'OMGs' around with wild abandon, not stopping to 'unpack' the expression (there it goes again)? I have certainly seen several high-profile atheists on YouTube using 'my god' in the course of conversations, so I tend to think it has become almost meaningless.

And what of the future? What if we fast-forward to a time when the current crop of gods have become historical curiosities, like the Roman, Greek, Norse and Egyptian ones are now? When people refer to gods such as Jesus with the same detached amusement that we currently reserve for Zeus and Apollo? Will there be new gods by then? Will the people of say, the 23rd or 24th century (or whatever they call their centuries), be still saying OMG! but be referring to deities we have yet to encounter? (Unless perhaps it's the one you have in your head which has somehow escaped).

Or maybe the increasing secularisation of western culture will ultimately lead to the end of religion altogether, when the supernatural framework that so many people use to make sense of their world is replaced by one of rational scientific enquiry. Then I feel we can reasonably expect the expression to disappear as well. Of course, it may be replaced by something a little more reasoned – just as language generally changes with new developments in society. What might our distant and more sensible descendants say? Maybe the expression will have evolved, and the equivalent of the Janice character will be leaning forward on the café sofa and squeaking something like 'Oh My Beautiful Natural World!'

I do accept a phrase such as this lacks the immediacy and punchiness of 'Oh my god!', but at least it has the advantage of being based on reality rather than illusion.

# Twenty-six - All hail to Lord Cod Almighty

Or is there something fishy going on?

15th August 2022

The previous article refers to the expression 'Oh My God!' and asks the question – which of the thousands of gods does this actually refer to? In the article I also made the point that as atheists often use the expression, the reality is that it has become meaningless.

But is it actually the case? As a committed non-believer myself (not 'atheist' by the way – why should I have to define myself by my lack of belief in other peoples' made-up concepts? I am just as much an a-mermaidist or a-unicornist) – as a committed non-believer, I feel deeply uncomfortable using that expression. If I find myself starting to say the words 'Oh my…' I stop. Maybe I am overthinking this (it wouldn't be the first time), but using a phrase that claims ownership of a god does not sit well with me. So I usually change it to 'Oh my goodness!' This has the benefit of conforming to my non-belief, but does also create the assumption that I have the 'goodness' referenced. And being English, my natural self-depreciation means this does not work too well for me either.

So I want to make a proposal – we should continue to use this phrase, but those of us who favour reason over faith should make one small change. Let's turn the 'G' into a 'C' – and solve all these problems in one simple stroke.

I can hear the cries even now. "Oh My Cod!" people say, "it's perfect! It allows non-believers to avoid being disingenuous, but it sounds almost exactly the same! So believers will think they heard 'God' when the non-believers know that's not what they actually said. There is no downside!

So that box is ticked – I shall now invoke my fishy deity 'Cod' whenever I encounter something extraordinary, amazing, or maybe even just a little odd.

But it has got me thinking – how might this Cod concept develop? What if I have inadvertently started a whole new movement; a new set of beliefs? Just as Christianity sprang into life from a few bronze-age stories then rode the socio-political wave to replace Jupiter and co, perhaps from this humble beginning, my Cod idea could do something similar?

Maybe we could imagine how a gullible society of the future might have replaced the current religions and worship Cod instead? Not to mention all the associated pomp and ceremony that could go with their beliefs…

...wavy fade into...

...It's 2,000 years in the future and the Chief Angler of England stands in his ceremonial gold waders and embroidered

Floppy Hat in front of his loyal congregation. Behind him are draped the iconic Fishing Nets made of finest silver thread, and above him is the magnificent carved effigy of Lord Cod Almighty, suspended by the mouth from the Most Holy Rod. He holds up a small rectangular orange object. "Lord Cod, you who were fished from the waters in order to save our Soles, bless this Holy Fishfinger. For us it becomes your body, dipped in breadcrumbs and fried in oil. Accept our offering, as we add your blood – the Holy Ketchup – to show our commitment to you, our Leader. Hook, Line and Sinker."

"Hook, Line and Sinker," respond the congregation.

Each member of the congregation then steps forward and grabs one of the gold ceremonial hooks that hang above them from silk lines, and allows themselves to be pulled up to the front of the church, where a series of beautifully made disposable-style barbecues are standing, on each of which is a silver frying pan containing many fishfingers. As each member of the congregation comes forward, an assistant Angler in silver waders puts his forefinger into the corner of their mouth, tugs it briefly and says, "In the name of the Scale, the Fin and the Holy Gill, you are hooked." They respond, "I am so hooked." He then hands them a fishfinger and a small dish of ketchup, saying, "Eat this in honour of Lord Cod Almighty. Hook, Line and Sinker."

"Hook, Line and Sinker," they reply, then dip the fishfinger in the ketchup and eat it.

Once this is finished and the congregation have all been pulled back to their seats, the Chief Angler steps up onto the ceremonial Three-Legged Stool, and begins his address. "My fellow Anglers," he begins, "I have to tell you that the Grillers, who would commit the basest heresy by grilling the Holy Fishfinger rather than Cod's chosen way of frying it, are attacking our faith at every turn." To groans from the congregation, he continues. "They have now issued an edict that the Holy Ketchup is not the true blood of Cod, but are saying that if you read the Scriptures correctly, Cod's blood was white, and it should be mayonnaise used in that most sacred of ceremonies. My fellow Anglers, we must stand firm in our faith! We must resist this heresy, and not be swayed by such dangerous new thinking!" He pauses. "In the name of the Scale, the Fin and the Holy Gill. Hook, Line and Sinker."

"Hook, Line and Sinker," the congregation replies.

# Twenty-seven - My Cod religion is a great catch

So let's not carp on about it.

22nd August 2022

The previous article introduces a possible new religion – the Anglers, worshiping a fishy deity, Lord Cod Almighty. Of course, what I didn't say, but I hope came through loud and clear in my article, is that I have already decided to embrace this new Angler religion myself. Hook, Line and Sinker.

When that article was first published on Substack, I had some comments from readers – one suggesting we should incorporate a role for Monkfish, and another suggesting it will never 'catch' on. One even told me they thought it was 'very funny'.

I'm sorry to say this, but I fear it is a sad fact that people are not respecting my new faith – and that is simply not acceptable. However ridiculous they are, my beliefs are honestly held - which means they must therefore be respected by everyone. Without question. You cannot go round suggesting that my belief in a scaly deity is in any way worthy of mockery. Or are you seriously suggesting that the Holy Fishfinger does not actually become the body of Cod, especially when dipped in His Blood (the Holy Ketchup)? Seriously? No. Exactly. It is quite clear to me that the holding of these beliefs is self-evidently reasonable. They are certainly no more fanciful than dying for a weekend to absolve people of the sins committed by a mythological couple and a talking snake, or all the animals in the world walking – some for thousands of miles – to reach a boat in the Middle East.

I reserve the right to be deeply offended by this lack of respect, and am sorely tempted to paint up a few badly-spelled placards and wave them in the general direction of those doubters and naysayers. I may even print up some bumper stickers saying things like 'My plaice is with Cod' or 'Don't flounder, perch on my Rod.' You know the sort of thing.

And what's next? Are these people going to stop me indoctrinating children with my beliefs? Kids' minds are like impressionable sponges, soaking up all they are told by adults. Scaring the kids, or as they are known in the Angler faith, 'Little Sprats', witless with my message of how unworthy they are of Cod's love is the best way to ensure the propagation of my religion. I relish the opportunity to traumatise them with my stories of a vengeful Cod rising up in the evenings from the Holy Stream and dragging them down into the depths if they are not good and observant Anglers. Not only does it ensure that Little Sprats grow up to indoctrinate their own kids, but it also reinforces brilliantly the point that Cod loves them. Deeply.

Indeed, I have a good mind to press the Government to have my beliefs recognised as an official religion. Then I can impose my creed on everyone else.

Where would I start?

Firstly I would make it illegal to eat caviar. Life starts at conception, so every egg in the sturgeon's roe is sacred to me. I cannot conceive that anyone would not understand this and accept that caviar would immediately be off limits. Any person - of whatever religion - caught eating the stuff, or even attempting to spread it on a little square of toast, would be guilty of a heinous crime and deserving of the full force of the law. What is more, to be caught in possession of a mother-of-pearl spoon will be considered absolute heresy. Such apostates will be punished by being hit on the head with a hammer and flung into a large net.

Next, I would enforce my strict dress code for women. Angling favours solitary men, who often use their religion as a way to get some peace and quiet – so my faith recognises this by requiring women to wear an appropriate outfit to demonstrate their acceptance that their men deserve unlimited 'me' time. They must therefore wear a full set of shapeless oilskins with white-soled yellow wellies whenever they are outside the house. Angling is a faith based on peace and love – and especially equality – so it is important that women understand this and know their plaice.

I would say to them "In the name of the Scale, the Fin and the Holy Gill, you are so caught."

Hook, Line and Sinker.

# Twenty-eight - King Henry VIII didn't believe me

When I told him his Church is no longer relevant

27th February 2023

Latest news; I have invented a time machine! I couldn't afford a Delorean, but fortunately an old Morris Minor became available, so I had a go. It was a little wheezy, and I had to lower the time-travel speed a bit, but it all seemed to be working, so I thought I would give it a test run. Being a Tudor history nut, I set the dial for 1545, then floored it. And boy, when that baby eventually got up to 38mph, there were some fireworks! I was whisked back to Tudor England in less time than it takes to say 'antidisestablishmentarianism'.

My sudden arrival caused some amazement, especially when I explained I was from 2023. This was considered sufficiently weird that old King Henry VIII himself demanded to see me. He particularly wanted an update on how his shiny new Church of England was turning out in 2023.

Sadly, the answers I gave did not please him at all.

"You mean to tell me," the King growled, "that less than half of the population of this United Kingdom identify themselves as Christian?"

"Yes indeed, sire," I replied. "We are what we call 'multi-faith', where we allow people of any faith – and those with none at all – to live side by side. So your Church has become smaller and smaller, to the point where it is only one of many Christian denominations." I paused to let him catch his breath, then added, "In fact, I am told that less than one in every hundred in the population regularly attend Church of England services."

"But your King is still the Supreme Governor?" he whispered, his face paper-white. "Like me?"

"Oh yes," I said. "Not only that, but even though your church has become such a small part of our lives, it still has a disproportionately high level of influence. In fact, twenty-six Church of England bishops still sit in the House of Lords, and are therefore able to affect laws for the whole population."

This seemed to please him. "The views of the people are, of course, quite irrelevant. It is the views of the elite, like Kings, archbishops and bishops, that count. If they say the edicts of my church are to be followed, then that is quite right and proper."

"Even when those edicts are increasingly at odds with the views of the people?" I asked. "And are expected to change at the speed of a glacier?"

"Of course. Such laws are the will of God, as defined in the bible." He gave me a puzzled frown. "So if the bishops demand people follow them, then it is because they are morally correct.

How is it up to the people to challenge this morality if it comes from God?"

"Because the morality of the bible is no longer relevant in 2023," I answered. "It may have been relevant as a means of social control when it was written in the bronze age, but we do not accept God's laws any more. Have you read the Old Testament?" I asked. "God is a homicidal maniac."

The King shook his head. "That cannot be so. God IS love, however many millions he might have killed." He nodded, as if convincing himself. "And the strength of faith is that it never changes. God's law was right in the first century and it will still be right in your time." He glared at me. "Or are you telling me that God did not create the earth, and with it Adam and Eve, in six days? Or that we are not all born in sin and need redemption?"

"Certainly," I replied. "In my time we have very learned men and women who have proven beyond all doubt that the earth is billions of years old and that all life has evolved over millions of years. And what is more," I added, "the concepts of sin and redemption are constructs of the bible. They have no actual, verifiable reality outside its pages. They might be useful to indoctrinate children and persuade adults to follow Christian laws, but they have no relevance in the real world."

"You lie!" the King shouted, his face now turning a deep red. "Have you no respect for the established faith?" Then he seemed to calm slightly. "And anyway, you say you have learned men 'and women'. How is it that women are learned? My wife Katherine claims an education, and it renders her most annoying; she is forever arguing with me on subjects she little understands. In truth, women are only good for one thing: making sons." As his face settled back into its more normal colour, he gave a rueful chuckle. "And they are not particularly good at that either."

"Women deserve every respect," I said levelly, trying to ignore his slur on Katherine Parr, "but faith does not. Faith is the belief in concepts that have no proof of truth or reality, so why should I respect it? And I may say, sire," I added, "especially not when faith is used to justify restrictive laws that affect other people. That may have worked in your time, but it is a sad anachronism in mine."

"I see," he said, considering me with a furrowed brow. "Then I must ask you, will my church survive?"

"I am not sure it will, sire," I answered. "It seems that our younger people are increasingly finding it perfectly possible to live their lives without the need for any religion – Christianity or otherwise. So in time, I think it will wither away. In the meantime, the rationale for an established church in the United Kingdom, especially one that represents a dwindling proportion of the English people, is becoming harder and harder to justify. The case for disestablishment is now overwhelming, and I hope that over the next few years, the church and state become fully separate."

"Never!" shouted Henry, as he started trying to heave his bulk up from his throne. I took this as my cue to leave before he decided to have my head lopped off – which I suspect was the only way he could answer the logic of my argument. That or tell me I am going to hell. Or maybe just pray for me.

I decided not to wait to find out, so I legged it back to the Morris Minor and fired her up. It was just in time too, as several guards suddenly appeared and started chasing me up the path. Thankfully I managed to reach 38mph just in time, no doubt leaving them standing bewildered in my scorch marks when I disappeared.

It was only after I got back to 2023 that I realised I should have stopped off for the winning Lottery numbers.

Ah well, maybe next time.

# Twenty-nine - Which way is your moral compass pointing?

Take this test to find out.

6th March 2023

A common moral framework is essential for a functioning society; without it we would descend into anarchy. If you don't believe me, try reading *The Lord of the Flies*, and you'll see where I'm coming from.

Back in the day, the moral framework was built around the dominant religion, and of course, in some countries it still is. But theological and political changes have meant that many societies, particularly western democracies, have evolved to a more humanist framework, structured around social democratic and political norms. And where religion once provided the glue that held the moral framework together (i.e. with the promise of heaven and the threat of hell), now we have police, courts and prisons in case we step out of line.

But do you believe that only the Christian bible can be the final arbiter of what is good or bad? How we should behave to eachother? Or perhaps you hold to a higher level of humanist morality based on common humanity and empathy?

To help you decide, I thought I would flex my creative muscles and put together a short questionnaire. Answer each question A or B, and then see at the end which way your moral compass is pointing.

## THE QUESTIONS

1. You are a famous sculptor. You have spent many days creating a large but very delicate piece. It needs to be taken to the gallery, which is across town from your studio, so you ask your assistants to put it in the lorry and accompany it on the journey. One of the assistants tries to steady it when the lorry hits a bump in the road. A piece of the sculpture snaps.

   Do you:
   A. Accept the assistant's apology; he was only trying to protect the piece from greater damage, and anyway, it's your fault for not insisting it was better boxed up?
   B. Take the assistant outside and shoot him?

2. A fight in a pub spills out into the car park; two men are throwing insults and punches. It starts to get very violent, and one man pulls a knife. The wife of the other man joins in, and manages to land a particularly accurate punch to the knife-wielding man's crotch.

Do you:

A. Offer to take the man to A&E, and accept that the wife was only trying to prevent greater harm to her husband?
B. Ask to borrow the man's knife, then take the woman to one side and cut off her hand?

3. You are the boss of a warehouse that packs goods. One of the workers refuses to obey an order by a supervisor. The supervisor then beats the worker so hard they have to go to A&E. Fortunately the worker is able to return to work after a few days.

   Do you:

   A. Fire the supervisor and report him to the police, then give the worker compensation, plus some extra time off to recover fully?
   B. Promote the supervisor to a managerial position for using his initiative, and praise him for stopping short of actually killing the worker?

4. You are a lifelong supporter of your local football team and have taken your son to every match since he was a small child. Now he is a teenager, he tells you that he wants to support the city's rival team, and wants you to come with him every week to their game instead.

   Do you:

   A. Tell him that you don't want to change your allegiance, but respect that he is old enough to make his own choices, then wish him and his new team the best of luck?

B. Take him outside and shoot him?

5. You are walking back from the pub one evening, when you hear some cries from an alleyway. You see a young man attacking a girl, and you believe she is being sexually assaulted.

   Do you:
   A. Pull the young man away, check the girl is OK, then call the police to come and arrest the man?
   B. Tell the young man that if he pays the girl's father £50 and promises to marry her, then that will be end of the matter?

6. You come down for breakfast one morning, to find your adult son is holding hands with another young man, and both are only in their dressing gowns. Your son introduces his friend and says that they spent the night together.

   Do you:
   A. Give your son's friend a warm welcome and make it clear he can become a valued member of your family?
   B. Take both young men outside and shoot them?

## YOUR ANSWERS

Let's start with **Bs**. Each of the questions provides a modern illustration of a specific verse in the bible that sets out a scenario and the legal penalty or God's sanction. So if you answered each question with a B, then you're a true follower of biblical morality! You are a religious pragmatist, and are not going to be swayed by all these 'woke' modern sensibilities – if the bible says it's OK, then that's good enough for you.

If you answered **As**, then your morality is based on common humanity and empathy. You don't need a bronze-age book to tell you right from wrong. Of course, you might also be a believing Christian – but you are able to pick n' mix your biblical morality, selecting only the laws that align with your values and those of the rest of society. You therefore recognise that this makes the bible effectively irrelevant as a sole guide to morality.

## DISCLAIMER & REFERENCES

As I am sure you have spotted, this is not a real quiz and I am not a psychologist, but this is simply an attempt at a (hopefully) amusing way to point out that modern morality must no longer be based on the bible. All the B. answers reflect some of the deeply immoral laws set out in the old testament, or the actions of the vengeful God character. I am sure these were relevant to the bronze-age society of the time, but they are clearly no longer applicable today. So if you claim the bible as a moral authority, you must either accept it in its entirety (answering Bs), or accept that it needs to be viewed through a higher 'humanist' filter (answering As).

# Thirty - The truth is out there...

You just have to find it.

6th February 2023

We live in an age where nothing is what it seems. Take a look behind any news article and the truth is often very different – if not diametrically opposite – to the story being told. This takes many forms – so please indulge me; I am going to take you from a trans woman in prison to the historicity of Christ via a holiday home – all to prove my point that you can't believe what you read in the news. Whoever said *5 Minute Break* isn't diverse!

Let's start with the story of the trans woman who was convicted in Scotland of rape before beginning their transition. This person was moved from a female prison to a male facility after an outcry. 'How can they be allowed in a women-only space?' was the demand, and one can certainly see the point. But, according to journalist India Willoughby, trans people, just like anyone who breaks the law, deserve to be sent to "a jail that is suitable for them, and where everybody else is safe." Willoughby says that this person was actually kept in isolation away from the other inmates, and was never allowed to present any real threat to their safety. She explained that [there is] "categorically no way someone who has committed rape would be moved into the women's estate".

Now I don't know, but it sounds much more plausible to me that a sensible decision is taken by a properly constituted board to keep a convicted rapist away from women, than there is some daft and blasé wokeness that allows such a rapist to self-identify as female, slap on a bit of lippy, then march freely into a space that gives them unfettered access to women. So when I read about the 'outrage' over this, I take it that it is the outrage itself which is the story, not necessarily the truth behind it.

But it's not just a modern-day issue. Here's a story from my personal experience, where the truth was completely different. Many years ago, my parents rented a small weekend flat in a coastal sailing town. Part of the rental contract was that each year we had to vacate the flat for two weeks, as it was already let to someone else for that period. Which was fine, until that other person suddenly became very, very famous. "London solicitor and family thrown out of flat by Mr X!" screamed the story in an outraged tabloid paper, making it sound like all this had happened recently, and only because this person was now very famous. If you strip away the embellishment, there was nothing there at all. But hey, never let the truth get in the way of a good story.

And we can go even further back in time to see that it has ever been thus. Early humans developed communities around shared stories, and it seems likely that these were embellished and grown by successive re-tellings, until they lost almost all contact with any original truth.

Nowhere is this clearer to me than the question of the historicity of Jesus. I think it entirely plausible that a mythological set of stories grew up around the exploits of various different mendicant preachers wandering around first century Judea with their bands of followers, all spouting their religious philosophies to the locals. And as these stories were repeatedly re-told, who is to say they did not start to come together into tales of a single preacher; one who became known as 'Yehoshua' or 'Jesus'?

Just like the story of the trans woman or my family rental, we can try to strip away the many layers of accumulated embellishments to see if there was any truth behind the Yehoshua story. Was there, for example, an actual person by that name, or even a single mendicant who did any of the things attributed to Jesus in the bible? Sadly, we can never really know, as we don't have any verifiable corroborating evidence outside the gospels (and even they are contradictory on several key points). That is because Roman historians, who were notoriously good at recording the major events of the empire, actually maintained a resounding silence on this particular story.* Funny, that.

So if you strip back the stories, did Jesus actually exist? Personally I think it is highly unlikely. The silence of the Roman historians speaks volumes, which leads me to conclude that the Jesus story has its origin in the tales that grew and developed from the first century mendicant preachers. Like the other news stories I mention above – but just on a much grander scale – the

* *Yes, yes, I know there was a first century historian who mentions Jesus; he was a Jewish chap called Josephus. But the passage that mentions Jesus was in a wholly different style to Josephus's and clearly inserted into a pre-existing section of his history. So it is generally accepted that this was actually a later Christian forgery.*

Good News does not really stand up to a factual scrutiny. I bet if you manufactured a time machine and went back to the right time and place, you wouldn't actually find a recognisable Jesus figure anywhere.

Incidentally, time travel and story-telling are devices I have used in my book, *The Witchfinder's Well.* My time-travelling character Justine arrives in 1565 from 2015 and early-on she says a four-word expletive. In time, after many, many re-tellings by Tudor-era folk, her few words have grown into a whole paragraph. I had a lot of fun with the idea, as each person sensationally adds more words as they tell the story. But the tragedy for Justine is that it is the final version which is used to substantiate the claim that she is a witch.

So we may live in an age of fake news and Photoshop, but boy, have we been telling whoppers a lot longer.

And that's the truth, believe me.

# Thirty-one - Faith Schools - a good education?

Discuss

30th January 2023

In Chapter twenty-three I set out what I saw as the compelling case against religion, and my own journey from being a young, casual Christian to being a rational secularist grown-up. While my parents had sent me to schools that were nominally Church of England, these schools had kept God and Jesus to within chapel services, rather than making them a core part of school life.

But what about Faith Schools, where Christianity or other religions are totally central to the school's mission? Around one third of schools in the UK state education system are classified as Faith Schools, and many parents have little or no choice but to send their kids to one.

So I wondered – what sort of education might I have had if I had gone to such a school, where faith is so fundamental to its ethos?

I googled a few and I found statements such as: "We do aim to deliver new skills and knowledge very much through the lens of the teachings of Christ" and "Christ is at the centre of everything we do." There's even one which I understand has a quote by the late Pope Benedict XVI as part of its mission – "We are not some casual and meaningless product of evolution. Each of us is the result of a thought of God."

I mean, what? WHAT? How on earth can you educate kids to be the next generation of scientists, leaders and thinkers that we so desperately need, while confusing their minds with such stupidity? Teaching them that they must not question religious dogmas, then (hopefully) teaching them actual proven facts? Thank goodness I didn't go to one of these schools! It defies belief (and I chose those words deliberately), to think what such teaching is doing to impressionable young minds. How much could it confuse them?

Let's consider some key topics:

**Scripture vs Science**

Do the kids go from a Christian scripture lesson where they are told not to question anything, to a science class where they are taught to question everything? Confusing or what? And does the science teacher explain that it is not possible to walk on water, turn it into wine, conceive without sex or rise from the dead… BUT, you can if you're good ol' JC, as the laws of biology, chemistry and physics don't actually apply to him?

**Sex and Relationship Education**

What are children told in these sessions? That the things society says are perfectly acceptable and lawful – such as sex before marriage, divorce and homosexuality – are actually 'wrong'? Does that come from the Bible? In which case (according to Genesis), incest is completely fine? And are they told that their sex lives (and innermost thoughts) are voyeuristically and intrusively monitored by Christ at all times, just in case they even think of straying? I must say, that really creeps me out. Might it do the same to impressionable young minds?

**Geology**

Do they learn that the accepted age of the earth is 4.5 billion years, or does the teacher make little 'inverted comma' signs when he/she tells them this, then add a little aside? Does he/she say that (according to the Bible) it was actually created by God only a few thousand years ago, and in just six or seven days? If so, I am sure the kids must also find this confusing and contradictory.

**Evolution**

Aha – the elephant in the classroom! How can the teachers reconcile the comprehensively proven scientific fact of evolution with their 'made by God' faith? Kudos to them if they find a way – perhaps someone could enlighten me?

## Thou Shalt Not Kill

Here's an interesting one. Do they teach the kids that murder is wrong, but point out that there's a 'get-out-of-jail' pass for the genocidal maniac that is the God of the Old Testament? Do they explain how this benign, loving deity laid waste to large swathes of the bronze age population for crimes like 'not believing in him'? And for crimes of general immorality, such as when he took out Sodom & Gomorrah? Or when he drowned everyone (apart from Noah) in the Flood? Are they told that he even bumped off Lot's wife, just for turning round? Do the kids get taught that while murder is wrong, all these ones were OK because they were done by God?

## Morality

Or maybe these Faith Schools just gloss over the shortcomings of the Old Testament God, and focus instead on the touchy-feely fluffiness of Jesus Christ? But – and it's a big but – there is also stuff here they'll need to gloss over as well. Such as the bit where Jesus says he loves you, but if you don't love him back, he'll torture you in hell forever. Nice. Or how human sacrifice and ritualistic cannibalism are central tenets of the faith. And do they acknowledge that Christianity is really a 'pick-n-mix' morality; where you use higher, non-Christian principles of human decency and empathy to select which bits of biblical teaching to accept and which to reject?

So I am left wondering how such Faith Schools square the circle, and teach kids on the one hand to ask questions that must be answered, while on the other hand telling them that there are answers that can't be questioned. It's not physically possible to do both, without compromising one or other. I fear that the schools where the ethos is such as "Christ is at the centre of everything we do", will sacrifice genuine education on the altar of their 'faith'. In which case I worry deeply for these kids, and for our nation's future.

In conclusion, whichever their teaching methods, I cannot see how any Faith School has a valid place in our modern society. Which is why I support the National Secular Society's No More Faith Schools campaign. And if you agree with me, please google the campaign website and add your support to this very worthwhile initiative.

We should be making sure our children get a proper education; one that equips them for life in the twenty-first century.

Not the first century.

# Thirty-two - There's always an easy way

If you want to consign religions to history

7th November 2022

I recently caught the final episode of a reality TV series where three members of the public pitched to become an 'alternative' UK Prime Minister. I accept that I only saw the final episode, so I never saw what the three candidates had to do to get into the final, but what they had to do to win it left me deeply saddened about the state of our country.

Each was asked to come up with the central plank of their policy, and put it to a vote by an invited studio audience. The candidate whose policy had the greatest resonance – and who therefore won the contest – was the one who said we should make corporations pay their 'fair share' of tax. The other two candidates offered to 'end institutional racism' and to 'end homelessness'.

Why did this leave me saddened? Because it gave the misleading impression that such deeply complex issues can be reduced to such simplistic statements. As if just wishing that things could be better would make them so, when the truth is that success in solving such problems would require equally complex solutions that could potentially in turn, create other – possibly worse – situations further down the line. And that's if you could even define what success might look like. It also saddened me that we are creating the perception that members of the public could do a better job than experienced politicians, who – whatever you might think of them – may at least have an understanding of the complexities of an issue (with, of course, some notable exceptions, eh, Liz?).

Yes, I know this programme was just entertainment. But what sort of entertainment is it that makes it seem that all our problems could be solved at a stroke if only a gung-ho member of the public could 'have a go' at leading the country? (Although with the way we're churning through Prime Ministers at the moment, maybe we'll all get to have a go before the next election). The truth is, of course, that there are no easy solutions, and at best, every policy is a form of compromise.

I know, it would be great if this were not so. If a Prime Minister or President could simply wave a magic wand and 'kazaam!' everything is made better. *The war in Ukraine*? Kazaam! The war is over! *Global hyper-inflation*? Kazaam! It's back down to below 2%! *Global warming*? Kazaam! Brrrr, it's cooling down! But that simply isn't going to happen, and giving us the impression that it might is to treat us as infants.

Of course, this brings me on to one of my favourite topics – religion… (*oh, no Jonathan – you're not back on that are you? Yep. Sure am.*)

I think that this reduction to simplicity that we see in the media has strong parallels with religion. Like religion, it treats us all as children (or sheep) who are hoping (or praying) for our leader (or god) to wave his magic wand and make everything better. And like religion, it suggests that there are easy answers to difficult questions. In politics this can be such as 'if only the other lot were in power, they'd sort everything out,' while in the case of religion, it could be, 'I don't understand the science, so therefore my god did it.'

The fact that religion treats us all as infants is self-evident to me. Why? Because it discourages questioning and independent thought; it asks us to believe in magic; it demands we accept its principles 'because I said so.' And most of all, because it begins its indoctrination at birth, making sure children have been exposed to all its teachings when their minds are most receptive. They are given a lot of contradictions (in Christianity at least); that they are 'born sinners' yet they can be 'saved'; that they are subject to 'god's plan' yet they have free will; that god loves them yet will burn them for all eternity if they don't love him back – and all this is thrown at them before they are old enough to question the nonsense they are being fed. So they end up as adults believing in stuff that they would never have accepted if they hadn't been force-fed it as impressionable children.

So here's what I would do if I were made the 'alternative' Prime Minister; I would make it illegal to indoctrinate any child into a religion until they were at least 18 years old. That would mean no baptisms. No Sunday school. No bar-mitzvahs. And definitely, DEFINITELY no non-consensual mutilations of their bodies by circumcision. I would protect their young minds and bodies from religious nonsense until they were able to make a rational assessment of what they were being taught. Then, once they were 18, their parents could sit them down and explain their religion. While I can't begin to assume that every 18 year-old will dismiss it for the guff it so patently is, I do think the majority will – and over time, religions will naturally wither away into the historical curiosities I think they should be.

Yes, it's a simplistic policy proposal. And no, I haven't worked out the details. I haven't understood the complexities – because in this world of simplistic solutions, it's the easy idea that counts, not the difficult implementation.

I thank you. I shall prepare my winner's speech in a minute.

If you have enjoyed these articles, you can see more on Jonathan's Substack blog '5 Minute Break'.

5 minute break

Life, the universe and other quick reads from author Jonathan Posner

https://jonathanposner.substack.com

# BY THE SAME AUTHOR

*When not writing weekly rants, Jonathan writes and publishes historical action adventure novels set in 16$^{th}$ century England.*

## The Witchfinder's Well Trilogy

### Part 1 - The Witchfinder's Well

**What if you fell through a time travel portal and landed in Tudor England?**

How long before you say the wrong thing to the wrong person? Before you're accused of being a witch?

For Justine Parker it's almost immediate. She hardly has time to find her feet in a historical world that's hostile for women, before she's on the run from a ruthless witchfinder. He makes it his deadly mission to submit her to a terrifying trial.

And if that doesn't kill her, he'll burn her to death.

Justine needs to do whatever it takes to keep out of his clutches. But she can't do it alone – as a stranger in Elizabethan England, she needs help. Handsome Sir William could be her saviour –

and even her lover – but his time is running out fast. A cruel twist of history says his own death is imminent.

Now Justine has to face a terrible choice – save herself, or change history and save her new love?

**Unless she can find a way to do both.**

From young adult to older readers, *The Witchfinder's Well* is a page-turning adventure packed with suspense, romance and excitement. If you like books like Outlander, the world of the Tudors, and strong female lead characters, discover Jonathan Posner's historical fiction series today.

**Readers have said:**

"*A must for everyone who loves history and a must for everyone who wants to be whisked away to another time.*"

"*An enchanting and un-put-downable read!*"

"*A good tale, entertaining, funny, informative, recommended, a good holiday book, one to go back to again and again.*"

## Part 2 – Alchemist's Arms

Lady Mary de Beauvais seems to be the perfect 16th century woman, but she hides a dark and terrible secret - she is actually a time-traveller from 2015. So when she discovers there's another traveller from her own time, she sets out across Elizabethan England to find him.

But it's a search that leads her into dreadful danger - threatening not just Mary's own future, but the life of Queen Elizabeth as well. So Mary is forced to face her fears and take control - if she wants to save herself and those she loves, in this "*gripping adventure thriller*".

## Part 3 - The Sovereign's Secret

Lady Mary de Beauvais's past finally catches up with her, bringing her to the attention of Queen Elizabeth's calculating spymaster, Francis Walsingham.

His daring plan then plunges her into a world of intrigue, espionage and danger.

Can Mary save herself once again, and in doing so, will English history have to change?

# The Lawyer's Legacy

**What if you uncovered a traitorous rebellion – but nobody believed you?**

**1535.** Tudor teens Ophelia Williams and Robert Wychwoode make a great crime-busting team. They've cracked open a Cornish rebellion against Henry VIII.

But when it comes to stopping it – then they're on their own.

There's no doubting their bravery. Or their relentless determination. Or even their cunning and ingenuity.

But will it be enough?

**Because the price of failure is death.**

*"...it kept me on the edge of my seat and I just wanted to keep reading. Couldn't put it down!"*

*"Most enjoyable Tudor historical fiction."*

*"This was a fun read, especially in following the escapades of a 16th century woman who learns espionage..."*

# The Broken Sword

**You only discover what dangers you can overcome – when you're tested to the limit...**

**Tudor England**
When Mary Fox is ordered to marry a sadistic older man, she decides instead to strike out on her own. As a woman in a man's world, no-one expects her to survive, but Mary is determined to prove them wrong.

Challenged to return the Broken Sword talisman and so break a centuries-old curse, she soon learns how to scheme, fight and outwit those who would drag her back to a life of servitude.

**And in doing so, she becomes more than a match for any man.**

*"Diabolically good! What makes this novel irresistibly readable is the emotional energy generated by the main character Mary Fox, her ups and downs, drawing parallels to our present times."* **Gina Flyvholm**

*"I would highly recommend this book for its entertainment, historical authenticity and value."* **Philip Appleton**

## The Tudor Prince

**Mary Fox is back. Her new all-action adventure lands early 2024!**

**What if you bear an uncanny resemblance to a kidnapped Prince?**

When 17 year-old Mary Fox is asked to impersonate 14 year-old Henry Fitzroy, the illegitimate son of Henry VIII, she is assured that nothing can go wrong. But she soon uncovers a treacherous plot – which it seems goes right to the heart of Tudor royalty.

And when a bitter old enemy turns out to be one of the ringleaders, Mary faces a desperate fight to get out alive.

---

**All Jonathan's books are available on Amazon and can potentially be ordered through your local bookstore.**

**For more information and to sign up for regular news, offers and sneak previews, visit Jonathan's website at jonathanposnerauthor.com**

Winter & Drew Publishing

winteranddrew.com

Printed in Great Britain
by Amazon

51658301R00091